D1029931

THE MAKING OF
OUTLANDER

THE SERIES

TARA BENNETT

DELACORTE PRESS | New York

THE MAKING OF
OUTLANDER
THE SERIES

THE OFFICIAL GUIDE TO SEASONS THREE & FOUR

St. John the Baptist Parish Library
2920 New Hwy. 51
LaPlace, LA 70068

The author would like to thank some important people for making this book possible. First and foremost, Diana Gabaldon for creating the *Outlander* world that inspires every creative decision in this TV series, and these companion books. My eternal appreciation to Ron D. Moore, Maril Davis, Matthew B. Roberts, Toni Graphia, Caitriona Balfe and Sam Heughan, and Sophie Skelton and Richard Rankin for their enthusiasm and time. I am beyond grateful for every minute they generously gave to this project; without them this book would not be what it is. My enduring admiration for the entire *Outlander* writing and directing team for providing unique insight about their creative process on this series. A hearty *sláinte* to all of the *Outlander* department heads, the production team, and every cast member who also provided such wonderful content inside these pages. Special thanks to all of the representatives of the cast for coordinating their clients to be a part of this book. Brad Page and Renee Fonmin for their invaluable help with the photography in the book. Virginia King, Gabriella Alaimo Thomas, and Rachel Addison from Sony for all of their support and chasing on our behalf. Louisa Radcliffe, Madeline Brestal, Ariana Rodriguez, and Nick Hornung from the *Outlander* offices for their coordination and behind-the-scenes wrangling to make everyone available to us. Huge love to my editor and creative partner in these companion books, Anne Speyer. She's always keeping me going with her virtual *dinna fash* messages of encouragement and support. To the *Outlander* fandom who made this second official companion book possible. Without your pre-orders, purchases and support, this sequel wouldn't exist. Your wonderful tweets, emails, and reviews are the wind under my creative sails. You are mighty and *tapadh leat*! Last, but never least, to my own beloved *cridhe* and *gràdh*, Paul Terry. Thank you for being my Outlander.

TM and copyright © 2019 by Sony Pictures Television Inc.
Introduction copyright © 2019 by Matthew B. Roberts

All rights reserved.

Published in the United States by Delacorte Press, an imprint of Random House, a division of Penguin Random House LLC, New York.

DELACORTE PRESS and the HOUSE colophon are registered trademarks of Penguin Random House LLC.

Printed in the United States of America on acid-free paper

Sketches on pages 116 and 192 courtesy of Jon Gary Steele

LIBRARY OF CONGRESS CATALOGING-IN-PUBLICATION DATA
Names: Bennett, Tara, author.
Title: The making of Outlander, the series: the official guide to seasons three & four / Tara Bennett.
Description: First edition. | New York: Delacorte Press, [2019]
Identifiers: LCCN 2019029192 (print) | LCCN 2019029193 (ebook) |
ISBN 9780525622222 (hardcover) | ISBN 9780525622239 (ebook)
Subjects: LCSH: Outlander (Television program)
Classification: LCC PN1992.77.O985 B47 2019 (print) | LCC PN1992.77.O985
(ebook) | DDC 791.45/72—dc23
LC record available at https://lccn.loc.gov/2019029192
LC ebook record available at https://lccn.loc.gov/2019029193

randomhousebooks.com

2 4 6 8 9 7 5 3 1

First Edition

Endpaper background image by iStock.com/Pierreot46

Book design by Caroline Cunningham

CONTENTS

SEASON FOUR

INTRODUCTION

By Matthew B. Roberts

Writer/Executive Producer/Director

In sitting down to write this introduction, I found myself grappling with some very particular questions. If Claire Fraser were to stop and take a moment to reflect on her journey from Scotland to the New World, what would she have to say? What thoughts would Jamie Fraser have to share about the trials and tribulations of forging a new life in eighteenth-century America? For those of us working in the writers' room, these are not unusual questions to ask at all; they are the sort of questions we are privileged to ask ourselves on a daily basis. The Frasers may be fictional, but they are alive both in our imaginations and on our screens. What *is* unusual, however, is that although Jamie and Claire have by now inhabited my daily thoughts for more than half a decade, they are ques-

tions I never could have guessed *I'd* be asking. How could I possibly have known, when I first encountered a book entitled *Outlander* during one of my first assignments in the industry, in my first industry job as a "reader," that it would play such a fundamental role in my career? But just as Jamie and Claire are destined to be reunited after twenty years apart, so it was for me. The stars aligned, and I found myself working as a writer/executive producer/director on a hit television show based on the very book I was once paid to summarize for ten dollars or so more than twenty years ago, and to which I "passed on"—on the grounds that the story and characters were far too rich and detailed to be encapsulated in the two-hour movie that my employers at the time wanted to make. My recommendation, instead, was that

it would make a fantastic television series.

In many ways, working on *Outlander* has been the fulfillment of a dream, particularly directing episode 313, "Eye of the Storm." Working in the capacity of director brought further dimension to the literal lens through which I engaged with the story: the words on the page realized before my eyes. Being so immersed in the varied stories and vivid landscapes, and coming to feel at home with the characters, often makes it tempting to find parallels between fact and fiction, themes that intersect with and echo in real life. In episode 401, "America the Beautiful," Jamie and Claire reflect on the vast, wild landscape stretching out before them, which will eventually become the United States of America. Claire tells Jamie that, in

time, people from every country in the world will flock there, "all hoping to live what will be called the American Dream." This raises questions for Jamie, who wants to know what that dream entails and if it is "the same" as their dream. Put simply, the Frasers' dream is to take advantage of the opportunities presented to them, their newfound freedom from the ties of the past, and to build a life and a new home together on the land granted to them in the New World. Although they know that doing so will likely be difficult, that they may encounter problems and pitfalls, and that perhaps there will be sacrifices to be made, they put their heart and soul into it. This is something that has resonated with me in more ways than one, and no doubt with anyone who has ever undertaken the immense challenge of adapting a book for the screen. Building a television show is in many ways similar. I use the word "building" here very consciously: A script is an architectural blueprint, the words on the page are carefully chosen and considered to support and maintain the structural integrity of the plot and its source material. Careful consideration is required in terms of design, decoration, and situation, much in the way that an architect works to create plans for a house. Each and every department collaborates to construct and design props, sets, and costumes. We too ask ourselves what materials we can use; what resources, talents, and skills we can draw upon; and what sacrifices might have to be made in working to bring a shared vision to life. We are grateful that there are so many who want to join us on this journey and make themselves at home in this story. We hope you enjoy learning, through this book, about the immense effort and the heart and soul that goes into it.

CASTING SEASONS THREE AND FOUR

For a casting director, when's the moment that they truly know they've done their job well? With *Outlander*, it came when the fans of Diana Gabaldon's books declared that they couldn't imagine any actors other than Sam Heughan and Caitriona Balfe as Jamie and Claire Fraser. For a fandom that had fan-cast their celebrity choices for two decades, that approval was a badge of honor for series casting director Suzanne Smith. And for four seasons, she's continued to achieve the right alchemy of pairing *Outlander*-verse book characters to real-world actors.

Yet even years into the process, Smith admits it hasn't gotten any easier. "It's an interesting task," she says, smiling. "Because every season we've got new things to contend with." In fact, since the *Outlander* pilot was made in 2013, there's been a wave of new television shows around the globe, draining the talent pool. In turn, it's forced Smith and her team to get even more creative about finding new faces.

"When we cast, we always try and look everywhere to make sure that we've covered everything," Smith explains. "You want different faces. We looked in Australia and that's how we found David Berry [Lord John Grey]. His Australian casting director did a little search for us." Smith also works with agents in European countries and the U.K. "The nice thing is every-

"We didn't do a chemistry read for Marsali and Fergus. We just went through with casting to find somebody who looked like Romann Berrux and I think we did that. I think César does look like him."

she says of the process. "Between [casting director] Simone [Pereira Hind] and myself, we talk about every episode. I tend to go up [to Scotland] for every script read-through, which is every block, or two episodes. We tend to sit down with Maril [Davis] and Matt [Roberts] and go through the characters that are coming up and how they seem, because they know the story so well and what they're looking for. It is a lot of talking, and sometimes it's just there on the page. You see it, and you go, 'Okay.'"

body knows what *Outlander* is now," she adds about actor awareness for the award-winning series.

With such an expansive array of characters to cast each season, Smith says, they've settled into a system that works for the show. "You have to have a good memory of the people you've used and that you're not going to bring back,"

"Ed Speleers is such a lovely person to play such a horrible man, with charm."

Smith reveals that for the series all actors audition for their roles, even Maria Doyle Kennedy, who had recently come off the cult hit *Orphan Black* and was cast as the much-anticipated Jocasta Cameron in season four. Smith says they were lucky to get her. "We were a good show for her to travel backward and forward, as she didn't have to spend a lot of time in one country and could be home. So sometimes you're lucky when it comes to casting and sometimes you're not lucky. You may fall in love with an actor and they say 'No,' because they have another job."

While every season provides Smith with unique challenges, season three for the first time required her to incorporate regional casting in another country, as the production relocated to South Africa. For all of the citizens of Jamaica and the West Indies isles, Smith enlisted the help of South African casting director Christa Schamberger.

Topping that in season four, Smith was tasked with accurately casting entire villages of Native American extras and actors for the Cherokee and Mohawk characters that would play an important part of the season. "We had Canadian casting director Jon Comerford help with the whole casting," she details. "I had worked with Jon before, and I chatted to a couple of Boston colleagues here and in America who had cast shows that had Native American or First Nations players,

"With Tantoo Cardinal [Adawehi], it was lucky that she happened to be able to make our [shoot] dates work, because she had a couple of other shows that wanted her."

asking, 'Where do you look?' [Producer] David Brown, myself, and Maril and Matt made the decision to go to Canada. Jon went around Canada to not just reservations but areas where there are indigenous populations. There's quite a lot of Canadian and First Nations actors who aren't in shows there, and they know who they are, so they brought them in."

Overall, the production needed to bring to Scotland at least one hundred extras, including men, women, and children. For the el- ders, there was the added issue of needing them to shave their heads to embody the traditions of the Mohawk people. "That was a process," she admits. "Maril and the writers prepared a breakdown of the characters, so we knew how many episodes everybody was going to be in. And then David, Jon, and I had the pleasure of choosing all the extras. We also had to find stunt guys as well. As it turns out, there were quite a lot of stunt guys who were on (Alejandro G. Iñárritu's) *The Revenant*."

SEASON THREE

BUILDING SEASON THREE: WRITING

There are things that every show shares—the long hours, the rewrites, and the difficulty of location scouting, to name a few. But what the creative team on *Outlander* discovered after two seasons is that their show will always be a beast to produce, no matter how well oiled the machine they've created. Diana Gabaldon's books get more ambitious with each entry in the series, featuring multiple time lines, changing eras, exotic locales, and an ever-expanding ensemble.

For the adaptation of *Voyager* as *Outlander*'s third season, the biggest decision executive producers Ron D. Moore, Maril Davis, Matthew B. Roberts, and producer David Brown made was to leave Scotland and relocate to South Africa for the last half of the season, a huge undertaking for any series to make. "Every year we try to come in more prepared," Maril Davis explains. "There's nothing better than having material early, but you can never prepare for the unexpected. Season three—perhaps at first we underestimated. We thought that, certainly, the move to South Africa would be daunting, but I don't think we realized how daunting it all would be."

"For instance, in the first half of season three, which I think is some of the best work we've done, we underestimated how difficult that would be, to do several different time periods," David Brown continues. "We had Claire back in the forties, fifties, sixties. Then, we had Jamie back in the 1700s. There were so many hair [issues]. Certainly, for Gary [Steele] and his team, it was an immense hurdle to have to keep changing the Boston apartment for each decade."

Although *Outlander* adopted cross-board shooting—shooting everything needed in blocks from any of the season's scripts, even if out of chronological order, to keep costs down—the coordination and scheduling was still massive.

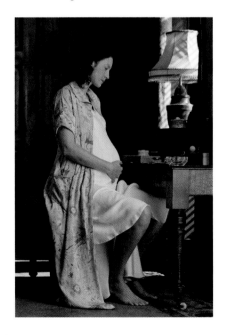

Behind the scenes, the day-to-day duties of the series also shifted. "The third season felt like the time to delegate more," Ron Moore explains. "I was definitely ready to stop being on the treadmill between Scotland and Los Angeles. It was time to give other people a chance to experience responsibility and authority and to come into their own. Matt, in particular, we started to give him more things to do, and Maril, and Toni Graphia. I think it creates, in the broader sense, a healthier business, because you're essentially mentoring and training people to discover their own talents and learn more. Then they can take that and make other great shows.

"So I knew at the outset that episode one of season three was probably going to be the last first draft that I sat down and wrote for *Outlander*," Moore admits. "That had a certain bittersweet quality

to it, but it meant I would spend more time in editorial and post-production in Los Angeles, which is one of my other great loves. Also, just generally speaking, I was starting to think about other [TV series] in development."

Davis then began to travel back and forth more from Los Angeles to Scotland and eventually South Africa. "Matt started spending most of his time exclusively in Scotland in season three and really kept that ship afloat there. My job does not require me to be on set, as we always have a covering producer. But I like to be on set, because I like to know what's going on. I deal with casting, publicity, directors, and writers. So having Matt there for me, and for Ron, is essential. He is operating in a director-producer-writer role."

As the man on the ground for two years, shooting second unit, problem-solving, liaising with cast

the official kick-off of season three. "We were shooting season two and they started a pre-room early to break down the book," Roberts explains. "So I was on the phone a lot and reading the [script] notes."

In the room, Moore, Davis, Graphia, and Roberts, initially remotely, were guiding the writing staff on how to dissect the big plot points from *Voyager* into the thirteen individual episodes for the season. From the top, they decided that Jamie and Claire would be in

separate times and narratives until the huge printshop reunion, which is beloved by fans of the books.

"Before the season even started, people were already asking the question of how long are you going to keep them apart?" Graphia remembers. "I would see people theorizing online. So we made the rule for ourselves that we will show them but never in the same frame. We wanted to do the sweet torture of keeping them apart for as long as we could. It's kind of the cardinal

and crew, *and* writing, Roberts was ready to invest even more, including taking point with David Brown on transitioning their team to a new country for several months. "Knowing where the story was going, we had already started to look way down the road, because we knew we needed ships and the Caribbean," Roberts says. "For the first half of the season, we knew that half of the stories would be in Scotland, and that was a great thing because we were in Scotland. But to make that even more challenging, we were going to [make it into] period Boston, which makes it more exciting."

Of course, before anything else, the *Outlander* writers' room convening in Los Angeles represented

rule of TV writing; you don't keep your leads apart. But we found a way to make the scenes about the two of them without having them both in the scene. We kept them alive as a couple even though they weren't together."

Roberts adds, "The only time we [broke that] was once in the very beginning, in Culloden, where Claire comes to Jamie in a dream, and that's it. We wanted the audience to wait for their big reunion, because we knew that was going to be the fulcrum of the season. The story really changes after that anyway. Getting back together is the first half. And then rescuing Ian is the second half."

"And we always planned the reunion to be episode six," Graphia clarifies. "I know that was way later than people were expecting," she chuckles. "Even the network was like, 'What do you mean, *six?*' I think they expected us to do it around three."

With the outline in place, Moore says, the writers then had to figure out how to show twenty years of living, on both sides, in the first five hours. "To separate these two characters and to move through this big chunk of time in their lives, every moment had to count," he emphasizes. "Every moment had to be chosen, not just because it was an interesting part of their lives, but because it also advanced the story and advanced the character's story along.

"The book neatly delineated Jamie's story into chapters," Moore continues. "Our first task when we sat down was, 'Let's start with the Jamie story, because those are each going to be an episode, and let's lay out those episodes.' Then we said, 'Now we need a Claire story that goes along with that,' and that was more complicated, because you were drawing from various sources and the time lines didn't neatly line up. You couldn't have the same passage of time in Jamie's world and the same passage of time in Claire's world. There was a lot of complexity to try to figure out how Claire's story would mimic in some way Jamie's story over these multiple episodes. That's what took the most work. The Claire story definitely got reworked several times, whereas the Jamie one was always kind of clear."

The writers also learned from their previous two seasons that they had to figure out how to honor Gabaldon's narratives but be confident to take their own story path sometimes. "The way Diana tells stories is different than the way you have to tell them onscreen," Roberts details. "An event might take place in the book, and Diana will skip over it in the moment. We can't do that. We have to tell it in the moment, or it doesn't play. So, those are the big things that we have to adjust. We also have to deal with other living people, who are directors and actors, and production designers, and costume designers, who bring in their own interpretation of things that are on the page. When you bring it all together, it's so collaborative. And there were multiple times we wanted to put people together and they just weren't available, so we have to tell a different story."

BUILDING SEASON THREE: LOCATIONS AND PRODUCTION DESIGN

Knowing that a large portion of Diana Gabaldon's *Voyager* was set in the West Indies and Jamaica, the producers of *Outlander* had a clear heads-up about their primary challenge for season three. So, at the end of season two, David Brown and Matt Roberts contacted their locations brethren to scour the globe for warm locales for their production.

"I looked at Malta; I was looking in the Caribbean itself; I was looking in Australia and obviously looking at South Africa," Brown runs down. "Weirdly, our relationship with Starz and the happenstance of *Black Sails*, and where they were in their production cycle, would enable me to deliver what we did in South Africa."

In 2016, Starz announced that its *Black Sails* series would come to

14

a close at the end of its fourth season, which meant its Cape Town sets and facility would be open when *Outlander* needed to shoot the blocks that would end season three. "They could clearly see the advantage of holding on to their resources they'd built up on *Black Sails* and letting *Outlander* have a go at them before they were slowly closed down," Brown explains.

"We went down there very early and we met with people," Roberts continues. "We scouted the ships and the studio. David went back again, and he started hiring crew."

Because Brown went to Cape Town nine months before the crew did, he was able to secure and coordinate all the details they would need far in advance. "I worked hard to get the *Black Sails* crew," he shares. "On the basis of that, we were able to make decisions to determine who [from Scotland] was going and who wasn't. We took only heads of department [HODs] and, for example, Gary [Steele] went out with Nicki McCallum,

> "There's a million things that happen on every episode that no one will even know that the team make look amazing. In fact, our whole department is amazing. Our construction, our plaster men, our paint, our scenic artists, our whole art department—they're all amazing."
>
> —Jon Gary Steele on his production-design team

our art director in Scotland. They did their initial designs, and we chose a location that the team in Cape Town were quite capable of carrying the mantle, and that informed stuff to do back in Scotland."

"Once [we] make the decision, then we go full steam ahead," Roberts adds. "And the first half of season three was great because it was in Scotland, so we used our studio."

After two years of using Wardpark Studios in Cumbernauld as *Outlander*'s base of operations, pro-

duction designer Jon Gary Steele now had four soundstages to build sets for season three's narratives. However, for budgetary efficiency, Steele and his team had learned in the first seasons to always craft and build important sets with the intention of repurposing them in future seasons. "With the [season two] apothecary, I knew the print-shop was coming. So, when we're building the apothecary, I wanted a second level on it. People were like, 'We don't need that,' and I go, 'Yeah, but I know what I'm doing in the next [season].' It saves you a lot of money by already having part of that built on another season's budget. Of course, it's completely redone, but we use the bones and the structure.

"Everything turns into something else eventually," Steele continues. "Every tavern will get turned into something else. Sometimes bedrooms get turned into something else. A lot of times we do it with tapestries on one wall; then you take them away and we've al-

"Culloden itself was a challenging location to find, in that there were various ideas that were thrown up. It was a logistical challenge in that we obviously had a lot of extras to get ready, and there was one location that we were looking at quite seriously but was quite a long way away. It was literally five days before we were due to shoot [the battle], and the location changed. I think it was the first location we shot of the season, so we were certainly thrown into the deep end on that one, and there was quite a lot of pressure."

—HUGH GOURLAY ON THE SCRAMBLE TO SHOOT CULLODEN

ready painted underneath to be the next thing. Doors and windows will swap out. It's like theater, for lack of a better way to put it."

One of the big standing—or nonmoving—sets for season three was Claire and Frank's home in Boston. Originally Claire and Jamie's Parisian apartment in season two, Steele and his team completely reworked it. "The whole concept was that as a professor, [Frank] tried to make it very booky, with lots of built-in bookcases," Steele details.

To create an authentic color palette for the residence neighborhood, Steele found car-color books from the period on eBay for inspiration. "We sat down and started tagging colors that I liked from that period because I wanted to play with those colors to be on the walls. We had tons of sea blues and greens throughout the whole apartment. You'll notice everywhere you look, it's different shades of blues and greens. And that was the direction that we went, with lots of wood and big staircases."

The Randalls' bedroom, Steele says, personified the shift in that marriage just with visuals. "When we were dressing the bedroom, I was sitting there with Gina Cromwell, the set decorator, and we're both on these twin beds, and I went, 'This is really a sad room, Gina. It's really depressing me.' And she goes, 'It's supposed to, remember?' So we laughed and went, 'Well, it works.' It was kind of down and depressing, and you try to evoke something with each set."

Working to match Steele's interiors to potential exteriors in Scotland was Hugh Gourlay, *Outlander's* supervising locations manager. Production ended up using the suburban streets of Glasgow for Boston in any exterior shots. "It's a city that's got quite a lot of brown sandstone, not as brown as Boston, but a reddish-brown sandstone," he explains. "It was in the west end of Glasgow we'd seen stuff that we liked."

For other locations needed in the countryside, or for locales like Helwater, Gourlay's department has built up a database of potential sites to film. And, surprisingly, their loca-

tion shoots don't garner the kind of attention that shows shooting in the United States attract. "In Scotland, *Outlander* doesn't have the presence and is not on everyone's mind as much as it is in America. So, when you're filming just off the Royal Mile, thankfully, that's not something that drew lots of people. If we were something that had much bigger awareness, it would have been a lot harder to manage."

Yet the series has created a tourist interest in many of the castles and areas they used in previous seasons, so Gourlay admits that many estates call him up now to offer themselves as a backdrop. "A lot of them will know other estates that we've worked with, so they'll be receptive to us. But equally they've also heard the difficulties, that you can then get potentially lots of visitors wanting to come and it can have a negative effect. But I think in the main it's a positive thing, and I get people emailing,

> *"The A. Malcolm sign had tons of images that were nods to Jamie being a Masonic [Mason]. It had Claire and Jamie's initials, different symbols of alchemy. We had tons of stuff in that."*
>
> —JON GARY STEELE

saying, *Why don't you come and have a look at this location?* It's nice to be invited. More often than not, their vision and our vision are two very different things, but you al-

ways wanna go and look, because you never know."

Case in point: Edinburgh's famous closes (or alleyways) are very busy tourist attractions, but one ended up becoming the exterior site of A. Malcolm's printshop. "It was logistically quite challenging, just because [of] parking, and we had quite a lot of extras," Gourlay says. "We also used another close just a little bit further up for a market scene we did. We were actually filming there quite often into the night, and one time we were there till three in the morning, which, being a residential area, is always slightly trickier, particularly when you've got mobile lighting platforms with beeps that you're not meant to be moving after eleven o'clock at night," he says sheepishly.

The printshop interior was built at the studios, where Steele and his team could totally control the iconic set for the variety of scenes needing to be shot in the space. "I wanted to have it on a couple levels with catwalks, to make it

> "We found research on a European printshop that had tooled-leather walls. We couldn't afford to do that, but in a few little scenes we had the graphics people do a mock-up. Then we printed it and stretched it out over all these panels. Then we bronzed all the moldings."
>
> —JON GARY STEELE

feel like a precursor to factories," Steele details. "I wanted to be able to see from one area to the next so that Jamie could see other people working in other areas, and Ron [Moore] said, 'Fine. Love it.'"

When it came time to shoot Claire entering the shop and seeing Jamie, Steele says, his intentions finally became clear to the producers, and it confused them. "At first, Ron and Matt both were like, 'You are putting them on two different levels?' And I go, 'Well, this is just an idea, but it's *Romeo and Juliet*. Imagine it's much more dramatic that she's up there, looking out the window, and

he's down there printing.' We had a model to show him and Ron went, 'Okay,' and Matt goes, 'It better be good, Gary,'" Steele shares, laughing.

For the overall aesthetic of the printshop interiors, Steele says, "When you first walk in the door, it's all built-in bookshelves, and one area that Claire walks to was Jamie's desk. We tried to show that he's an educated man. There were books everywhere, and books were really expensive at that time.

"As for the color itself, it's basically blood red," Steele continues. "We had not used red anywhere before. Especially in season one, we

could never use red, as that was only used for redcoats. I wanted to use that for the fact that it conveyed danger and risk. Jamie's obviously not afraid of really anything. He's doing these covert printings. So I thought, this is a chance to use red.

I asked Ron and he said go for it, and I think that's the only time we've really done it."

When director Norma Bailey's episodes completed shooting, Matt Roberts says, the Scotland production went on hiatus for a month to transition the cast and partial crew down to South Africa. "We moved most of our HODs and our cast down there," he explains. "Then we used the South African crew, who seamlessly started working with us. It was a beautiful mix; they were so welcoming to us and they really wanted to do our show. When *Outlander* comes to town, it's not a small thing. It's great on everybody's résumé."

"We'd traveled outside of Scotland before [Prague, England], but we'd never relocated the producer to another country for the length of time we were in South Africa. The undertaking of that kind of move was enormous," Maril adds. "God bless David Brown and his crew for pulling that out. Our Scottish crew doesn't see much sunshine. I've never seen so many sunburns in the first few days," she laughs. "You also have to imagine two and a half seasons of intense, harsh, rainy, cold weather, and then we took our crew into a place where the median temperature was eighty degrees and sunny every day. But it is because of the crew's planning, and the fact that we have a lot of experienced people who know that that kind of move isn't easy, that the payoff just was seamless."

> *"We used the Signet Library in Edinburgh for the interior of the Governor's Ball in Jamaica. That was quite challenging because, again, just the number of extras. We had to get all the extras in costume and makeup down in Holyrood Park in a bus on the Royal Mile."*
>
> —HUGH GOURLAY

It also allowed Steele and his designers, and then the South African construction crew, to build environments never before seen on the series. "We completely redid whatever areas *Black Sails* were filming in, because we didn't want it to look like their show," Steele details. "Everything was re-painted. We built one whole ship interior."

He continues, "We built Geillis's house with a reflecting pool of blood onstage. We made the walls look like they were sweating, for lack of a better way to put it. The colors were almost like fuchsia, but grays and blacks were coming through. It was like it had been painted many years ago, and the humidity made the colors change and pop off. It was a fun set to do and it turned out pretty cool. And the exterior was on a location in South Africa."

And as is the way with *Outlander*, while the crew was busy in Cape Town, Steele and the remaining Scotland departments were already working on season four.

> *"Cape Town Film Studios had a great back lot, where we built Father Fogden's huts. We built that onstage and [then] parts of it on the back-lot location. We built a forest with forty or fifty palm trees, and all kinds of vegetation, that created the pathways for when Claire is working her way through the jungle. The Cape Town greens department was amazing."*
>
> —JON GARY STEELE

EPISODE 301: THE BATTLE JOINED

WRITER: RONALD D. MOORE DIRECTOR: BRENDAN MAHER

When it came time to draft the episode that would open *Outlander*'s third season, Ron Moore knew that it would have to finally deliver on the Battle of Culloden. The fateful conflict was heavily foreshadowed in the season-two finale yet not explicitly detailed in Diana Gabaldon's *Voyager* prose, and Moore

made the showrunner decision to actually show it. "The series had been talking about the battle for a long time, and it was baked into the mythology from the books," Moore details. "When you translated that to television, it had the effect of just teasing the audience. We felt like we had to show it."

In researching the history of

the battle, Moore discovered that the whole clash took only about twenty minutes. So his initial thought was to re-create it in real time. He explains, "We'd go beginning to end and frame it through the eyes of Jamie and Murtagh. The first draft of the script I wrote did exactly that. I walked through the major elements of the battle, Jamie's

"I hadn't really worked out
what my expectations of [Jamie
and Jack's ending] were.
We don't have very long to land
the end of that story, and I'm
not entirely sure how you do end
that story. Where do you go?
As always with the Jamie and
Jack stuff, you're looking for a
slightly unusual angle on it.
Not just the straight-up two guys
go at it and one of them dies.
I liked the way it was built into
this hallucinatory sequence of
Jamie remembering fragments
from the battle and it's buried in
there. I like that it was a strange
dance/fight/embrace. It felt
in keeping with what's come
before. It's a hard relationship
to type, really."

—TOBIAS MENZIES

perspective coming back after he took Claire to the stones, and then his interaction with Prince Charlie and participating in the final charge. I sent that to production, and, essentially, we couldn't accommodate it on our budget and our schedule. It would have put us deeply, deeply in the hole for the entire season and really crippled our plans for everything else that we wanted to do."

Going back to the draft, Moore assessed the key moments that needed to be shown in Jamie's story. He decided, "If I can't show the whole [battle] in a linear way, then

"I really like the execution of
the Highlanders in the cottage
and Rupert's death. I thought
that was moving and wonderful.
Sam did some amazing work,
when you consider that he had to
lie on his back and basically
couldn't move through all those
scenes. I just thought he was
heartbreaking in his reactions
to Rupert's death."

—RON MOORE

probably the best way to do it is to make it more surreal and subjective, with an impression of moments, and make it more emotional, more intimate, and see it through Jamie's eyes. When you're just fading in—it's all over and Jamie's lying on the battlefield, near death, having these memory flashbacks—you can just convey an emotional experience of battle. That's essentially what we ended up doing. And all the moments that are in the [final] episode are part of that original, first draft."

Veteran television director Brendan Maher, known for his work on action series like *Strike Back* and *Spartacus*, was brought in to open the season's episodes. For Culloden, Maher says, his primary focus was on "the scale of the battle and what was happening in Jamie's life. It was about capturing Jamie in a very intimate way in this huge landscape. We couldn't lose track of

what his story was. He had a leader's jeopardy on him—not just his own survival but the survival of his troop."

Maher praises the production crew for how they rallied around the intense logistics needed to pull off the Culloden sequences. "You don't do that battle sequence by yourself," he enthuses. "I loved their work ethic and their human and creative talent. Scheduling this movement of people and equipment, on and off the set, in various ways, is huge. We had between two hundred fifty and three hundred [background] people, so just to get them costumed and ready every morning was a huge exercise."

For the mêlée scenes, Maher praises the work of the stunt team, as well as that of Heughan and Tobias Menzies (Black Jack Randall), who did all of their fighting sequences. "They were on their feet

fighting for days," he details. "It was just an exhausting, mammoth task for them, and they were terrific. Their work ethic was outstanding."

In particular, Maher has high praise for their climactic fight. "When they see each other for the first time on the battlefield, in complete stillness, you can see the passion, the hatred, the sense of what's gone on before and what's about to happen," the director explains. "It was the climax of this piece. We set out to make it look like it was sunset. We blocked it roughly with Sam and Tobias, but it was an open ending. There was this big, heroic feel to that sequence, but in the end it's pathetically, exhaustingly, human. And it's about who can take the last breath, because they are both going to want to deliver the death blow."

Moore wasn't on set the day that scene was shot, but he relates

> *"There are two young boys that are going to be executed. They're beyond hope, upset and scared. They're behaving as they should at their age. One of the characters says, 'Keep your chin up, do your best,' and they come out. One of the clerks asks them for their name, and we talked a lot about the weight of your name. I still get emotional about it. These young actors, they just got it, you know? The scene starts with them in tears, vulnerable and hopeless, and they leave the scene walking toward their death, full of pride and dignity. That little moment, I think it's gorgeous. I really love it."*
>
> —DIRECTOR BRENDAN MAHER
> ON HIS FAVORITE SCENE

how impressed he was with the delivered footage and performances. "Toward the end of their fight, there's a moment when Black Jack reaches out and touches Jamie with his hand. That was something I'm pretty sure Tobias came up with on the day. They did it in one or two takes. I saw it and I loved it. I was like, 'Oh my God, that's perfect.'"

The other half of the episode's narrative was far less physical but no less dramatic, as Claire and Frank try to restart their marriage in Boston leading up to the birth of Brianna. For Moore, crosscutting the parallel stories across time became the model for the first half of the season. "It established the language that we're going to go through, literally, twenty years of these characters' lives and we're going to do it in this structure, which was a pretty unusual thing to do," he explains.

With the Randalls' story in particular, Moore says, it "was an opportunity to cobble together a lot of different things that had been mentioned in various memories and flashbacks scattered throughout Diana's books about the relationship between Claire and Frank."

In just a few short sequences, Maher says, Balfe and Menzies were able to speak volumes about the fraying relationship. "Emotionally, I think, Claire feels very imprisoned in those sequences," he muses. "I thought Caitriona was fantastic in the scene in the university with the dean. She's all the

things that Frank wants of her, and he knows how difficult it is for her and how grateful he is of that. But through her smiling, polite gentility, he can see how she's seething with discontent. How she hates being locked into this world. And you're waiting for a moment where she's gonna explode and say, 'This is just not for me at all.'"

"I liked the idea of starting their story in the most optimistic moment in Boston, a new house, a new beginning, pregnancy," Moore adds. "I loved the way Claire and Frank walked through the house, being a little playful. I really wanted the audience to be rooting for them. There was a hopeful quality to their relationship that you held all the way to the end, until the moment when that nurse says, 'Where'd the red hair come from?' And that breaks it."

SPOTLIGHT

CAITRIONA BALFE AS CLAIRE BEAUCHAMP RANDALL FRASER

Just as Claire Beauchamp Randall Fraser has lived a myriad of unexpected adventures by the end of the first two tomes of the *Outlander* book series, so too has life imitated art for Caitriona Balfe, the actress playing Claire in the television series. With the international success of the TV adaptation, Balfe, along with her co-star Sam Heughan, was swept into the frenzy of constant fan and media attention as they traveled the globe promoting the series. And the work itself, for each of four seasons to date, has earned her Golden Globe nominations for Best Performance by an Actress in a Television Series–Drama.

All of the work, the press, and the attention were a lot to navigate for an actress top-lining her first television series. But by season three, Balfe found some equilibrium. In playing Claire for two years, Balfe had weathered the demands of multiple years of Scottish location shooting, assuaged a fandom with huge expectations that she was

the right actress to play the beloved character, and crafted a nuanced portrayal of a woman experiencing such intense love and loss that it shattered the boundaries of time.

Balfe admits that she embarked on the third season of the show with a modicum of ease, due to known expectations. But the narrative that opened the season with pregnant Claire relocating to Boston with Frank Randall (Tobias Menzies) in 1948, while Jamie lives through Culloden in 1746, did not fall into the same category. It was unique.

"It's such an evolving show," Balfe muses. "It never really stays in one place, and our characters, especially in the beginning of season three, were going to have such a journey through time. I think having those challenges always make you feel a little bit like you're starting fresh."

The actress says the start of the season in particular required a lot of prep work for Claire. "We knew that

don't necessarily agree they would have stuck it out if it was *all* horrible. So it was fun to try and find those times where the respect and the friendship take precedence over the lack of passion."

While die-hard worshippers of Jamie and Claire often express consternation about any screen time given to Claire and Frank, Balfe says playing that was incredibly important for her to create the woman who would eventually find her way back to Jamie.

"I definitely feel like Claire had given up this huge part of her life, but at the same point, humans are incredibly resilient," she explains about her mindset for Claire. "To the best of her knowledge, Jamie was dead. Claire's a widow, and the grief that you hold in your heart when somebody that you loved so dearly and had such good memories with—that's so much easier to carry than to think that there is somebody out there that you love and you just can't be with them. I had to make that distinction, because that completely changes how you progress in your life."

With the Randalls' marriage failing, the shift in Claire's focus provided Balfe a rich well of experiences to play. "Claire has so many other things in her life that are wonderful things to live for, her daughter being the primary [one], but also her career. She had these great

Tobias and I had this relationship with Frank and Claire, [told] with really short moments, where we were going to get to try and tell the full story of a twenty-year relationship. That presented quite a few challenges, but it was also part of what's so great about this show. It really presents you sometimes with a puzzle that you get to work on trying to construct well."

Reuniting with Menzies once again, she says, was a comforting place to return to. "In season one, two, and three, we always start with Claire and Frank, so that was quite familiar territory. Tobias is such an incredible actor, and he and I actually really relished creating this very complex relationship between Claire and Frank. That relationship in season three was so compromised and it was so complex, but there was still love there."

Regarding the task of portraying the arc of their marriage in just three episodes, Balfe says, "The difficulty was finding the moments where they do connect and being aware where they have comfort in each other. Because there was one thing that we both were very adamant [about], that we didn't want to play twenty years of misery, because I felt that that would have been a real point of weakness for both of those characters. I

outlets to channel her energy into. I also think because she had felt a love so deep and so overwhelming, in many ways, that was enough for her for a lifetime. She was quite happy in some ways to shelve that side of her, because even though she was a young woman, I think she knew that she would never find anything comparable again."

Due to the guest-actor logistics in season three, Balfe reveals that she finally reunited with Sam Heughan as a scene partner in the second block of shooting for the episode "First Wife." They were separated again for another block before they came back together to play out the much-anticipated printshop reunion in "A. Malcolm"—a book moment arguably as revered as the wedding. Balfe says figuring out how to portray their reunion spurred many intense creative conversations. "When we were talking about it, we all didn't want it to be the classic romance-novel moment. But I think [fans] were dying for Jamie and Claire, the second they saw each other, to just strip everything off," she laughs. "But what the writers and Sam and I all discussed, and really wanted to work on, is the fact that these are two people that haven't seen each other in twenty years. They have been building up this image of each other and, in many ways, creating this fantasy of this person who existed for them. It's such a potent and important moment in their lives, and you have to break through that fantasy, and you have to take people off the pedestal to be able to fully connect again. That was a really interesting journey for us."

She says they all worked to make sure it would come across as a credible moment, certainly soaked in their chemistry but also reflecting the reality of the situation. "We wanted to play with it like they were two teenagers again and do some mirroring to 'The Wedding' episode.

And even though they've never forgotten about each other, they don't really *know* each other, so there's a process of discovery. They aren't quite sure what to do with their bodies or their words. I think that lends a realism to it."

Balfe says she was grateful the writers gave her and Sam so much vulnerability to explore. "Of course, there's that initial bolt of recognition and there's no doubt that they still love each other, but are they the same people that they loved before?" she queries. "That's a very valid question to pose, and that moment when they look at the photos [of Bree] and they get to share with each other these other places in their hearts, that is very important. Now Jamie's a father and she's a mother. Life has brought them in very different directions. You have to explore all of those little parts before they can give themselves to each other again."

From the reunion on, Claire and Jamie's story progresses from Scotland to Jamaica in typical whirlwind Fraser fashion, with all kinds of high drama including kidnappings, shipwrecks, and even flat-out fights between the couple.

Balfe admits she especially loved those moments of conflict. "We ... show this fantasy of this aspirational relationship, but we have to ground it in as much truth as possible for people to really believe it and get invested in it. I think sometimes fans want more fantasy, but I think if we gave it to them, they wouldn't enjoy it as much. You have to be a little bit cruel to be kind," she says, smiling.

Shooting the last episodes of season three on location in South Africa was also a huge departure for the series, as they had previously shot only in the United Kingdom and Prague. Balfe says she was deeply appreciative of the weather that welcomed the cast and crew in Cape Town for three months.

"Sunshine is a really big help when you're tired and outdoors a lot," she chuckles. "South Africa was amazing. We were very fortunate to be with my closest team

members, Marnie [Ormiston], my costumer, and Anita [Anderson], who's my hair and makeup. I rely on both of them so much for so much support. It was great to have them, but we missed a lot of our crew. We've become so close with them. But to do something different for us—and it was such a visually different experience—it does invigorate you again. When you are in a routine year after year, it definitely helps sometimes."

The change of venue also served as a natural transition point for the story line, which by season's end would put the Frasers in the colonies of America for the fourth season of *Outlander*. The cast and crew returned en masse to their Glasgow warehouses and studio to shoot Scotland for the east coast of colonial North America. "It was amazing when we finally came back for season four," Balfe enthuses. "Ninety-five percent of the crew have been there since season one, which is incredible."

Interestingly, Balfe admits that season four is the one she likely didn't think enough about going into production. "Claire has always been reactionary in many ways due to circumstances in her life," the actress explains. "I always said that she was a compromised

woman last season. And it's funny sometimes when you get presented with these new opportunities to look at a character in a new way; it can be surprising.

"[Season four] was a complete shift, because for the first time, I think ever, I was getting to explore this real, nurturing side of Claire," she continues. "That's not necessarily the accurate description, because to be a mother you have to be very nurturing, but I think it was a self-nurturing that we never got to explore before. And to explore the value of her being a wife and what that meant to her, and creating a home and what that meant to her: In this modern time, we tend to sometimes neglect the value of that as well, and it was nice to be able to look at her in that way. I feel like this is the culmination of many sides of Claire getting to finally come together."

Some may assume that playing the domesticity and happiness would be easy, but Balfe admits it wasn't. "I'm not gonna lie—in the very beginning it did feel a little odd," she laughs. "It took a little bit of recalibration on my behalf to just wrap my head around 'this is who she is this season and this is what she's working on,' because she's *not* working on it. *I* was working on it."

But what was easy for Balfe this season overall was having more scenes with Sophie Skelton as her daughter, Bree, and watching her work together with Heughan. "I love working with Sophie," she says, beaming. "I think she's such an incredible young woman, and she's a real great asset to our cast and to our set, because she's just phenomenal. It was really nice to watch Sophie and

Sam get to play out this very paternal relationship. It was interesting to watch that dynamic and to see him have to learn that to parent at [her] age is very different than if they were children. You really see the difference between Jamie and Claire and how they handle those moments, and it's because Claire's had that experience of raising Brianna since birth."

EPISODE 302: SURRENDER

WRITER: ANNE KENNEY DIRECTOR: JENNIFER GETZINGER

"Surrender" provided audiences an intimate look into the respective day-to-day lives of Jamie and Claire living apart. In 1949 Boston, Claire is raising baby Brianna with Frank. Jamie, in 1752, exists in a solitary life spent hiding in the Fraser woods as an outlaw under the name Dunbonnet/Red Jamie.

Former *Mad Men* director Jennifer Getzinger joined the series to

helm the Lallybroch episodes for the season, which meant produc-

tion was back on location for a time outside Edinburgh, at Midhope Castle. "We definitely went a lot grittier for Jamie's [scenes]," the director explains about their aesthetic for shooting the Fraser sequences. "We did more handheld things and just really wanted to play with the roughness of the way he'd been living. And then with Claire and Frank, there is that great feeling that there's this façade of a happy

"Living in that marriage,
she did make overtures to try
and make it work on a level that
she could. Obviously, that didn't
work out. And resentment and
bitterness does come in any
relationship that's not
functioning. You see, for both
Frank and Claire, the price that
they've had to pay for ignoring
certain sides of themselves."

—CAITRIONA BALFE

home, so we did things much more lyrically with them and tried to make everything look beautiful."

A palpable ongoing theme in the episode is how often Jamie and Claire are thinking of the other. Each is like a specter dwelling in the periphery of the other's life. Getzinger used that yearning as a transition between time lines. "I definitely was always thinking of how do you get from Jamie to Claire?" she explains. "We were trying to do something where they were never together in the episode, so we asked, 'How do we make it *feel* like we feel their connection?' A lot of times we would try to end the scene on Jamie's face and then start the next scene on Claire's face, like a vision, so it almost felt like they were together."

Without Claire in Jamie's life, his sister, Jenny (Laura Donnelly), steps up to prompt her brother to come back to himself. Getzinger

was deeply impressed with how Heughan and Donnelly played their scenes together.

"The two of them have this great brother–sister chemistry," she praises. "Jenny's so tough-talking with him, but there's such a connection there, and there's really this great warmth. She loves him so much, but she just wants to grab him and shake him and be like, 'What the hell's wrong with you?' half the time. They're really good at playing that stuff. We always leaned into really finding the moments of warmth, because we just didn't want all [that] she was doing was nagging him. It was always important to find the moments where you could see through what the nagging's about."

Interestingly, Getzinger explains, they ended shooting the Jamie sequences with the cave scenes. "They had to actually build that cave from the inside of it and the outside of it. We had picked a

spot in the woods that looked like a cave could be coming out, but there was no actual cave. The art department had to really create that and then also create it in a clever way that we would be able to build the inside of it on set. So, we had to give our department time to create that."

For the Boston scenes, the writers' room wanted to make sure that the episode allowed Frank's

disconnection from his wife to be as sympathetic as Claire's longing for Jamie. "Maril and I had a lot of discussions, because we really loved Frank," executive producer Toni Graphia details. "We know that the fans are not as keen on Frank, but it's always been our assertion that we love Frank because of how much he loves Claire and that if Claire hadn't had this other man, who's such a good man, it would be such a slam dunk for Jamie. And we wouldn't love Claire if we felt that she was mean to Frank or using

> *"[Laura] had actually just had a baby in real life and then had to go through the process of pretending to have a baby. She was a trouper about it. And if anything, I think it actually really lent such an authenticity to it, because the memory of what it really is was so visceral for her."*
>
> —DIRECTOR JENNIFER
> GETZINGER

Frank. We wanted to build a strong triangle where there are a lot of gray areas, so we really relished delving into the whole Frank relationship."

Getzinger concurs, adding, "Frank was really, really deeply in love with her. She was the love of his life, so I liked being able to show his side of it in a vulnerable way too. He gets angry, and he gets a little mean when he's angry, and you see this ugly side of him, but I think you also saw the wounded, good person side of him. For Tobias, it was just tracking exactly where he was and how much was he trying. She is trying too, but she's so lost in

> *"What I've really enjoyed in season three is especially when he's with Jenny and when Jamie isn't really speaking much at all. I tried to get the writers to cut a lot of Jamie's dialogue, so he's sort of monosyllabic and really barely able to speak because of his grief. That for me was fun and interesting to play, and they did cut a lot of dialogue."*
>
> —SAM HEUGHAN

Jamie and in being in love with somebody else that it never feels really real, and she can't force herself to make it. She is almost trying to force herself to make this marriage into something more than it is, and she just can't do it."

"We got to explore another side of Jamie. It felt like he went on this real dark journey to discover who he was, and he didn't want to be himself."

—SAM HEUGHAN

Playing out their scenes in this hour, Getzinger says, is like the "last gasp" of Frank and Claire's relationship. "It's the last try, and then by the end, that's it. It's really done by the end of that, and they're in separate beds."

SPOTLIGHT

SAM HEUGHAN AS JAMES ALEXANDER MALCOLM MACKENZIE FRASER

How do you embody a character crafted to be a paragon of manhood? From the first instance that Diana Gabaldon introduced James Alexander Malcolm MacKenzie Fraser on the page, he's been embraced by readers as the pinnacle of all things fine and good in his gender. Even *Outlander* series executive producer Ron Moore coined him "the king of men."

Those accolades are more for a god than a man who possesses human flaws and frailties. And that is why, in the four seasons of playing Jamie Fraser, actor Sam Heughan has leaned into the parts of his character that make him more relatable. Those choices have only attracted audiences more to the actor's fierce yet sometimes heartbreakingly vulnerable take on the character. Over the course of fifty-five episodes, from "Sassenach" to "Man of Worth," Heughan's performance has swept audiences along with him as he makes real the

journey of Jamie Fraser into the man he's destined to become.

Looking back, Heughan is thoughtful about his character's arc. "I think it's really interesting that season one was this young warrior, and he has no ties. And then he becomes a husband and then a leader of men. A clansman. A chief almost, and he's growing up. He's not as tempestuous; he's not as hotheaded, maybe. He's aged. There's now experience, and that's nice to watch Jamie trying to build the foundations for his family and a place for them to be. But also to take a back seat a little bit and try and guide younger members. But it's *Outlander*, so he's always there, as there's always some drama," he notes with a smile.

Indeed, the Jamie that audiences met in season one at Castle Leoch is certainly not the same man building his own homestead at Fraser's Ridge in season four.

had a very different energy on set." But it allowed him to play Jamie letting go of Claire more authentically. "When he finally does say goodbye to her, in a way he finds a little bit of peace and a new life in England, working as a groom."

In the episode "Of Lost Things," Heughan appreciated getting to work with an almost entirely new group of characters and showing Jamie in such a paternal light. "We get to see Jamie be a father, for a short time. Finally, he gets the one thing he really wanted. [He and Claire] had a child before, Faith, which was really heartbreaking for the couple and their relationship. But now he finally has a child. He yearns to be a father figure to him, but he can't directly do that, but he's very proud of Willie."

Though Heughan is not a father, he says he looked to his life to help inform how he played scenes between Jamie and Willie. "I thought a lot of my relationship with my father," he shares solemnly. "I didn't really know him that well, and it wasn't until the end [of his life], but I met him."

What he pulled from that was an intention for Jamie to be a guide, and a friend, to Willie. "Jamie knows he'll always be there for Willie and always love him, so it's heartbreaking when Jamie has to leave him. But he

Heughan's been able to translate his six years of filming the series into a significant gravitas for a now twenty-years-older Jamie. Some of the most extreme years of his life are portrayed in season three, in the years after Jamie survives the brutality of Culloden. Heughan calls the season his favorite because of the long path back to himself.

"He goes through this battle, and he wakes on the battlefield, but I think he expected to die," Heughan muses about Jamie's plight in "The Battle Joined." "He has to live now without the woman he loves. He doesn't want to be Jamie Fraser anymore. The grief has really taken over him. He's like catatonic in the first few episodes, a shadow of himself, living in the memory of Claire."

The Dunbonnet, Mac Dubh, Red Jamie. Even Alexander Malcolm. "Each episode, he assumes a different identity," Heughan points out. "It's quite a journey. Every episode felt very different, and it was wonderful to play Jamie struggling to find a reason to live. And then when he does, it's about other people. It's about living to help his family, his extended family, and to help his men as well when he's in Ardsmuir prison."

Heughan admits it took a bit to sort out playing without Caitriona for so long. "It was odd, actually. It

Heughan says it's the fulfillment of a dream for Jamie, who's only wanted a hearth and home to call his own. "It's the beginning of a new chapter for them," he says of America. "And it's also a new chapter in their relationship. There's no longer that 'will they/won't they' be together thing. They're very strong in their relationship with each other. They're at peace, I think, with a harmony between the two of them. There's a great joy to that."

However, playing that sense of peace, initially, was surprisingly disconcerting for Heughan and Balfe. "At times we were worried that maybe just them being so settled with each other would not be interesting to watch," he laughs lightly. "But, actually, I think it is. You get to see them interacting with each other and be quite domestic. Seeing how much they work together and know each other, without having to talk or having to discuss certain things. I enjoyed those moments with [Claire] at Fraser's Ridge, when they're at this new cabin. I think it's nice we get to see another side of them."

Season four also brings Jamie full circle with his lost fatherhood, as both Willie and Brianna come back into his life. With Willie, "Blood of My Blood" affords him a moment to get reacquainted with the growing boy he entrusted to John Grey to raise. And in the case

leaves him with someone that he really trusts, and that's also the beginning of this great relationship with John Grey. There's this mutual understanding between the two of them."

Jamie's slow exit from Helwater is a crushing visual, but it metaphorically washes the slate clean for him. Having experienced the ultimate losses of Claire and Willie, Jamie moves forward—and unknowingly back into the arms of his beloved wife in "A. Malcolm."

Seeing Jamie's reaction through Claire's eyes in "Freedom & Whisky," and then through his own in the next episode, really lands the momentous event. "It's like the first time," Heughan says of Jamie's dramatic reaction. "He's absolutely delighted that she's back. They've missed out on a lot. They've missed twenty years of being together, so there's a lot for them to get over. They've both had different experiences, and, ultimately, they aren't still the same people, yet they still have this great love for each other."

Despite the trials and tribulations of getting to know each other again, Jamie and Claire prove their love on the journey to Jamaica. Even when both are threatened with mortal danger and are separated on multiple occasions, they survive it all, including the wrath of the sea, by sheer force of will. When they wash ashore together on the sands of Georgia, it is their new beginning to carve out a life side by side, once and for all.

The Frasers begin season four with the intention of laying down roots for their family for the first time.

of Brianna, he gets to meet his grown daughter with Claire, something he never expected to experience.

Heughan says Brianna's appearance in "The Birds and The Bees" is the true catalyst of the season for Jamie. "You see in her the intelligence, the fire, and the humor of both [of them]," he explains. "You see what the character actually gets from Jamie, but you also see the side that she gets from Claire. And it's a complicated relationship that Jamie has with her, obviously, with Frank being the father. She really sees Frank as her father as well, so there's this feeling in Jamie that he really wishes he had had an influence on her life. In fact, that's why he [chose] America. Before she's there, he's trying to help mold this land, somewhere in the future, that has been a great place for her to live."

It's Jamie's immediate protectiveness for her that spurs him to beat and sell Roger Wakefield to the Mohawks when he first arrives on Fraser land. "It's Jamie's fire for his seed that makes that happen, but actually it's a misunderstanding," he says a bit sheepishly for his character. "And it's the deep memories that he has of what happened to him with [Black Jack] Randall, and everything comes into play there. It's like an old fire that's ignited in him, and I think Roger is lucky that Jamie doesn't kill him. [His anger] does get him into real problems. He's a father figure, but yet there are still moments when he has these failings and he doesn't think. But it's great to see [Jamie] in trouble," he jokes.

To Jamie's credit, when he

learns of Brianna's true assailant, he embarks to New York to find Roger and make things right, which essentially puts the Frasers back on the road to danger once more. Heughan chuckles. "I don't know what it is about the show. It's just so full on and pretty relentless. It's like shooting basically four movies back-to-back. It's neverending. It's like going through quite an intense experience."

But, he's also grateful to continue to do it with Balfe by his side. "She's incredible," he says with sincerity. Over six years, they've been constant scene partners, buddies in press tours, and friends. That has created a unique bond that Heughan says "definitely has changed and grown. We definitely know how each other works. I push her buttons, and I think she knows how to push mine," he laughs. "It's like a marriage, in a way. I'm just so lucky."

With fifty-five hours of Jamie and Claire's story revealed by the end of season four, Heughan admits with a bit of awe, "It's hard not to constantly look back on experiences and what we've done before. Even this

week, I was back in Scotland for a couple of days for [costume] fittings for season five. Being in the studios brought back memories of starting and discovering and trying to explore who these people are, why they are. I've made two movies over this break, but nothing compares to *Outlander*."

EPISODE 303: ALL DEBTS PAID

WRITER: MATTHEW B. ROBERTS DIRECTOR: BRENDAN MAHER

In the parceling out of writing assignments for season three, Matt Roberts remembers, no one was eager to take possession of "All Debts Paid." "I don't know why it shook out in the room that nobody was really digging the episode, which had Frank dying and Jamie in Ardsmuir prison. But I was like, 'I'll take that one!' It was one of my favorites to write and build; I really like that one."

The narrative was again split between eras, with the Randalls in 1956 Boston and Jamie "Mac Dubh" Fraser serving out his prison

term among his Scottish kin in 1755.

Roberts says he liked playing with the inversion of Jamie and Claire's troubles. "The pain factor was pretty high for Claire, but for Jamie, it was kind of counter to that," he explains. "He was finding his footing again, a little bit. If you look at the episodes prior to that, Claire was finding her footing in becoming a doctor. She was learn-

ing to live again while Jamie was suffering through those two episodes. Here Jamie's finding his footing, becoming a leader of men again. He finds his godfather and he makes a new friend. But because of how *Outlander* works, we ripped that all away from him at the end."

Director Brendan Maher returned and, through Jamie's sequences, continued to tell the story of post–Culloden Scotland. "Every man in that prison is emotionally in prison," he muses. "John Grey is in prison. He has been banished, put out on this moor and sent to prison because of his background. Jamie is in emotional prison. He doesn't want to be there at all. In a way, I think Jamie would have been really happy to have died at Culloden.

And Murtagh is imprisoned emotionally as well. Not only because he needs real help, but he's really aware that this culture, everything about his life, it's coming to an end."

The story also continues the strange intertwined destinies of Jamie and John as they reunite in the prison, years after Jamie spared the young John Grey's life. As their friendship grows, Grey initiates a moment of potential intimacy toward Jamie, which echoes experiences in Wentworth Prison many years before.

"I thought that the sequence where Grey exposes his love for Jamie is handled incredibly low-key and there's no high dramatics in that scene," Maher demurs. "It's got real weight because of Jamie's background with Jack. It comes out of nowhere. It's shocking and revolting to Jamie. It brings up the brutality of what he went through with Jack, as he is in prison, locked in, with the potential for it to happen again. The simplicity and the

> "John Grey is a great ally of Jamie's and a great intellectual. They enjoy each other's company, and I think have this mutual understanding. [They have] discussions and they play chess; I think that's very much their relationship. It's very thoughtful and slightly political. And I think John Grey definitely uses Jamie at times. And likewise they're constantly playing against each other. But they're equals. I think they're on opposite sides, but yet they are drawn together. It's great."
>
> —SAM HEUGHAN ON JAMIE AND GREY'S FRIENDSHIP

pain of John's rejection was really great."

In the Boston time line, Claire and Frank's marriage increasingly sours the older Bree gets, with Frank asking Claire for a divorce so he can relocate and marry Sandy. Maher loved how that breaking point

played out. "He walks down the hall to get car keys, and she's left in the room by herself. You've got them looking at each other, and there's a need for approval, and they both feel for each other deeply, but they've both got this wall between them. There is love there, there is understanding, but this wall between them is Jamie. Cinematically, visually, I think that's really nicely realized."

That moment is followed soon after by Maher's other favorite scene, when Claire tragically says

"I really liked where they are at the kitchen table and Frank's making breakfast for Brianna. It's quite a modern thing, because for Frank to be the primary caregiver in the fifties is a really forward dynamic they've created. I loved that you saw they have many mornings where they talk about what's going on in the papers."

—CAITRIONA BALFE

goodbye to Frank's deceased body. "It's a simple shot that is the last shot of that episode, where she walks down the hall," the director explains. "She gets to a door and half her face is masked and half is realized, so you can only see one eye. And you get the [question] of which Claire are you going to get: the hidden half or the open half that we know about? She then takes this really confident but frightened step through the door, and I just thought that was a nice bit of visual storytelling of where she's at."

Roberts concurs and adds of the moment, "Claire has this heart-break that is freeing her, because all the guilt and all the pain that she suffered being with Frank is now gone. She can just focus on truly loving Jamie solely again, even though she doesn't have him. I think it somehow frees her in that moment after Frank died. You can see that she's really torn up about his death, but she played it as she walks through the door that a new life is on the other side."

"It was actually my idea giving him Sandy [Sarah MacRae]. I was interested in exploring the tragedy that there is a woman out there who loves him and wants him badly, rather than Frank is a man with needs so he goes out and gets his needs met. I came at it from Sandy's point of view, which is, 'I found this great guy and I want him. I could've made him happy, but his heart belonged to another woman.' This is not in the book at all, and that was one of the things that was most fun for me to write. From the beginning of the season, I had in my head where a woman comes to [Claire] and essentially says, 'Why didn't you let him go?' We really show the selfish side of Claire, that she loved another man and has no right to be jealous or possessive of Frank. But we did protect Claire in that we made it very clear that this was Frank's choice."

—Toni Graphia on the genesis of the Sandy character

BUILDING SEASON THREE: COSTUMES

When it comes to categorizing *Outlander* as a "costume drama," that term has always been taken very seriously by the series. Led by the talents of Emmy-winning costume designer Terry Dresbach, the first two seasons of the series presented viewers with a visual feast of

> *"It was a very interesting thing for me to design that period, because I know it. I lived in it. It's the first time I've designed my childhood."*
>
> —TERRY DRESBACH ON COSTUME DESIGNING FOR BREE IN THE LATE '60S

era-accurate design, colors, and engineering. Whether scenes were set in Scotland, Paris, or 1960s America, Dresbach and her team recreated it all, sometimes in bulk, to bring the world of Diana Gabaldon's *Outlander* to life onscreen.

As discussed in depth in the previous companion book, the first

two seasons of *Outlander* were grueling in terms of building up the infrastructure to realize the ambitious costuming needs for the series. But those years did yield much wisdom and experience for Dresbach's team, which helped them plan more efficiently how best to execute seasons three and four.

"They really gave us a blueprint," Dresbach says of the previous seasons. "So in the middle of season two, I started designing season three, and then I could use my experience in one and two as my jumping-off point. What I knew—and this is the tremendous advantage of knowing the book—is that we were going to America. And in [season] four, I knew that was going to be an enormous build for our team that would be almost identical to season two in Paris. So when I approached season three, I knew

that [the characters] were mainly on ships, and I could use that [extra] time for season four." With entire colonial towns and Native American villages to dress on the horizon, that calculated redistribution of time was vital to pull off what was coming in season four.

Aside from the extra-heavy season-opening Battle of Culloden, the next major costuming narrative came with the Frasers' sea voyage to Jamaica. "You're limited in how many clothes you're going to have

> *"People still aren't catching that Jamie in season three is wearing his suit from season two. When you're designing for* Outlander, *what's really, really exciting and fun is that you can design for the third and fourth watching. You design with the assumption that on the first watching, they're just paying attention to the story. And then, the second and third and fourth watching, they'll notice the darning on Jamie's lapel."*
>
> —TERRY DRESBACH

Jamie
Fraser
Ridge

Claire
Voyager
S3

- Grey suit
  made from
  60's raincoats
- waistcoat
  - secret pockets
- Bree's house
- belted with
  arisaid
  (on ship)

"Other than Master Raymond, I don't really believe in symbolism in clothing. I'm not sure where that came from, but it is a dialogue that's out there. [People ask,] "What is the meaning of blue?' There is no meaning to blue. It's just blue. But I did break that rule with Brianna at the funeral service. I did have Jamie and Brianna in very similar-feeling clothes in that episode because it was the first place, with Frank's death, where I really wanted to break free and establish a connection between the two, between Brianna and her biological father. But that is probably the only place in the entire show I did that."

—TERRY DRESBACH

on that ship, especially when the decision is made at the last minute that you're getting on it," Dresbach says, smiling. "You're not bringing twenty-five thousand costumes. It's not going to make sense story-wise. And then we have no idea, in real life, what the conditions of shooting are going to be, except that your lead actors, and everybody else, are going to be sliding around a wet ship in who knows what kind of weather. So here is where reality

and the story support each other. If we had been shooting Versailles on a wet ship, we would've had a problem. But we were not doing that, so it allowed us a break so that I could design a minimal number of costumes."

With the macro view explained, Dresbach refocuses on the design challenges that took most of her attention in season three, particularly how Jamie and Claire visually transitioned through clothing back to each other in "A. Malcolm."

For her team's part in supporting that arc, Dresbach explains, "I always say, 'My job is not to design clothes; it's to design characters.' If

the actor cannot lose themselves in the clothing and transform into a new person, then I'm not doing my job right."

A big part of that is the historical accuracy of the garments, which Dresbach often makes the foundation of her pieces in both design and usage. "We were able to really settle into a little bit deeper research at this point, seeing how people use clothing," she continues. "In real life, people [at that time]

Brianna
Frasers
Ridge

- read through
  - men's wear
  + women's
  combined
- 70's feel !!

Young Ian
Frasers Ridge

Brianna
1970

- Indian Gauze
  mini dress
- Brown suede
  "car coat"
- Guatemalan
  Bag
- Frye boots

"I did everything possible to put every favorite outfit I had from about the age of seven through to 1970 on Sophie. I literally re-created my clothes. I had a leather suit when I was eleven, and I searched high and low for a leather suit for Brianna and found one. But it was just too far and too distracting. But her costumes have been some of my favorites."

—TERRY DRESBACH

Adewehi
Cherokee Nation

only had a few items of clothing. And they wore things, and wore them, and wore them, and wore them, and repaired them, and re-wore them, and darned them, and patched them. It was an opportunity for us to really dig into that, which I remain utterly fascinated with and we carried through the two seasons."

With that in mind, Dresbach started with Jamie, who went from almost-dead soldier to living in a cave to finally coming back to humanity on the Helwater estate. "His clothes are given to him, as he's a groom, so he matches everybody else. And then, when he gets to Edinburgh, he gets what was left of his old clothing, out of the trunk at Lallybroch.

"With Claire, she's a modern woman in the sixties, so she's got a modern wardrobe," Dresbach continues. "That's not one or two outfits—that's fifteen, or whatever, and that was a blast. It was about eighty percent vintage, bought on various Internet sites. Some pieces were a hundred eighty dollars, and some pieces were eight dollars. We just picked what was right for the character, and it was quite the luxury, because the ancient-history costumes are so costly. Suddenly, looking at a coat that's two hundred fifty dollars, it's like, 'Oh, that's so cheap!'" she laughs.

"And we ended up with way too much stuff, because it was all fit to

be Claire as a doctor in 1968," she continues. "I really used some of my teachers as the examples. In 1968, I think I was around nine or something, and my teachers were the working women that I observed. Blouse and skirt and sensible pumps were the order of the day. Then throw a doctor's coat on over it."

When Claire decides to go back in time to find Jamie, she has to create an outfit that will serve her well for the time and her travels, unlike

Claire
Graduation

- Silk shantung
  2 pc. suit
  celery!
- matching
  pump
- jeweled
  brooch

Nawohali
Cherokee Nation

that white shift she wore through the stones in season one. Gabaldon details the travel frock specifically in *Voyager*, and Dresbach went all out in creating a real version for Caitriona Balfe to wear.

Dubbed "the Bat Suit," as inspired by the functionality of the Caped Crusader's utility belt, it became the much-talked-about Claire costume of season three. Dresbach explains: "Before it was called 'the Bat Suit,' I called it her Salvation Army costume, because I was trying to design something from the viewpoint of a fifty-year-old woman who was going to time-travel back to meet a man in the eighteenth century; she had no idea if he still loved her or whether or not he had moved on. She had no idea. I needed

something that would reflect that place in her life but then create a bridge to when she and Jamie really reunited.

"And as a costume designer, I wanted to devise something where, on set, they could decide it was gonna be whatever anybody wanted it to be," she continues. "I'm thinking about slippery boats. I'm thinking about cold weather, and wet, and rain. I'm also simultaneously trying to figure out, what is a costume that will serve all needs? Something that has to be just incredibly practical. The idea of that suit is that it was many, many layers. And I didn't care if you wear

the waistcoat here and don't wear it there. Do what you will with it."

Dresbach says she remembers those early days working with Balfe as it evolved in fittings. "It was really difficult, because Cait and I were both like, 'Uh, this is interesting. How is this going to work to wear this for essentially a season?' It was not easy, and it was difficult until we got to the place where those layers started to come off. And then, I think, Cait could find Claire again. I was taking her *way* outside of her comfort zone, saying, 'Be uncomfortable. Be awkward. Don't wear something beautiful.' But then we were gonna journey back to that. Back to the comfort, and back to her sexuality, her sensuality and love."

And in a truly full-circle visual, when Claire is shipwrecked on the beach, the suit is stripped down to a white shift once more. "When she's wandering around that beach, she's taken all the way back down to where we started on the show," Dresbach says with pride. "It's funny: [The suit] ended up being one of my favorite costumes, be-

cause it really sends home the point that I want the audience to under-

stand, which is that costumes tell stories, and if *that* costume doesn't tell a story, *no* costume does."

Dresbach ended up handing off the final layers of the suit to assistant costume designer Nina Ayres, who traveled with the pared-down filming team to South Africa. Meanwhile, Dresbach stayed in Scotland to prep for season four.

> *"The black dress with the white lace that [Bree] wears at Frank's service with the green plaid cloak over it was in the September 1968 issue of Vogue magazine. I will never forget [that issue] as long as I live. I found two [copies] and it had that dress in it. I remember it also had a section on the Highland swing, these little plaid outfits with little caps. I would have crawled across broken glass for that dress. My mother got it for me for Christmas. And I wore it until she finally said, 'Okay, it's really way too short. You cannot do this.' But that is the velvet dress that Brianna wears."*
>
> —TERRY DRESBACH

EPISODE 304: OF LOST THINGS

Writer: Toni Graphia Director: Brendan Maher

As the next two episodes were broken in the writers' room, Toni Graphia found herself desperately wanting to write some of the seminal scenes that ended up landing in each. "Usually, we don't have writers write back-to-back episodes, because it's a lot of work," she explains. "But I could not choose between them. It would've been a Solomon's choice to give up one or the other, because

> "Right before Lady Dunsany gives Jamie his freedom, he looks down at the baby and says, 'You're so wee' and 'Dinna fash. I'm here.' It makes me cry."
>
> —Toni Graphia

one was mostly about Claire and one was mostly about Jamie."

Ultimately, Graphia loved both

and decided to write each script because they thematically worked as a matched set, as "Of Lost Things" is about fatherhood and "Freedom & Whisky" is about motherhood.

"In 'Of Lost Things,' its heart and soul is that Jamie becomes a father," Graphia explains. "Even though he's had Brianna, Jamie doesn't know if Claire made it back to the future. And he doesn't know if Brianna was born safely, espe-

cially [because Claire had] lost Faith. So this is really where he becomes a father for the first time and gets to see Willie as a baby and be in the first six years of his life."

The path to fatherhood comes via Lady Geneva Dunsany (Hannah James), who blackmails Jamie to lie with her to avoid losing her maidenhood to Lord Ellesmere. Graphia defends Geneva, a controversial character in the book, as a product of her time. "She's forced to marry someone she doesn't love and, ultimately, you understand why she does it."

Director Brendan Maher concurs, adding that their intimate scene allowed the vulnerability within her to finally come to light. "Leading into the lovemaking scene between Jamie and [Geneva] set up this woman as mean and forthright and spoiled. There's a nastiness to

> "I think in the book Jamie prays to the Virgin Mary, but I'd already used the Virgin Mary in 'Faith,' because [the] Madonna is a symbol of Claire and her motherhood and losing Faith. So I used Saint Anthony in 'Of Lost Things,' because he's the patron saint of lost things and both Claire and Jamie had lost each other and lost their children."
>
> —Toni Graphia

her. And then in that scene she says, 'I don't know what to do. I'm really scared.' I thought that sequence was really nice."

The idea of sacrifice is also deeply ingrained in Jamie's journey as he spends years in service at Helwater. "First he has to sacrifice

his home, Lallybroch, because he's given freedom at the same time he's given his son," Graphia says. "He chooses to forgo his leaving Helwater to be in his son's life the first years, so he sacrifices his freedom, literally, which to Jamie is everything. And then he sacrifices his son because he realizes once the

they don't function very well. We talked a lot about this, just from a technical point of view, on how to convey a really well-articulated internal life while onscreen.

"And I loved his work with the young boy [Clark Butler]," Maher continues. "Toward the end of the episode was just phenomenal. And just so simple. He's just full of love for this boy, his son. But, of course, he can't tell the boy anything about that. I loved how they built this unexpressed love, but you can see it

child is old enough to be recognized as possibly belonging to him, he doesn't want to ruin his life."

"I loved Sam in this episode," Maher says with sincerity. "I think it's one of his best episodes. I thought Sam was incredibly brave in his performance, where everything about him and who he is as a character—his soul—has to be hidden. He can't tell anyone who he is. He's a rebel, and he has to suppress that. I think when anybody's creativity or who they are is suppressed,

"Before I even started writing 'Of Lost Things,' I had the Bob Dylan song in my head because, to me, the song is about fatherhood, whether it's about individual fatherhood or fatherhood of a country. So I played it on a loop when I was writing. But I thought, We'll never be able to afford Bob Dylan. While I was writing that episode, Bob Dylan won the Nobel Prize and I remember thinking, No. Now his price is gonna go up for his song! But our script coordinator actually sent me several cover versions, and one of them was the band Walk Off the Earth. When I heard that one, I knew that was the one, because it's a duo of a male and female singing the two parts, and I thought, Ah, that's Claire and Jamie. That's the male and female perspectives that we kept cutting to in the show. I wrote it for the montage at the end because I thought, Everybody's losing something. Claire is losing hope to find Jamie. Jamie's losing his son. Roger's losing Brianna."

—TONI GRAPHIA

clearly with everything he does with that boy."

"That last scene where he rides away is just one of the most heart-breaking things," Graphia sighs with emotion. "Sam did a great job in the scene where Willie runs toward Jamie as his heart's breaking. I thought that was one of those magical episodes that just came together."

"You see for the first time each of them in isolation as they're parting ways. It's such a nice moment, because you see Roger with his toy plane. In that moment, you may think he's lusting for Brianna, but he's not. If you think about everything that has happened to Roger, that little scene says a lot about where he's at. He's not sitting there pining for Brianna. He actually just sat thinking about his dad, and him as a boy, and what that house meant to him when he was younger. And all that loss."

—RICHARD RANKIN

EPISODE 305: FREEDOM & WHISKY

WRITER: TONI GRAPHIA DIRECTOR: BRENDAN MAHER

Having laid out the twenty-year story of Jamie and Claire's lives apart, it was time to bring them together—after one last important goodbye. In "Freedom & Whisky," Roger's proof that Jamie survived Culloden causes Bree to give her mother permission to go back through the stones to find him. For

writer Toni Graphia, that was the crux of the entire episode.

"Maril [Davis] and I, more than anyone on that episode, had a lot of discussions about what it means to be a mother, and we didn't want to shortchange that a woman should be able to do what she wants and not be completely tied to her kids," Graphia details. "We really felt strongly that the only way to do that story and allow Claire to go back was if it was all right with her daughter. It's something Diana [Gabaldon] just didn't explore in the book, and we really wanted to dramatize that and make that the decision."

After Frank's memorial, Brianna takes the moment to allow her mother to follow her heart. "She was the one who rose to the occasion and said, 'I want you to go. I want you to go be happy. It's your turn,'" Graphia says. "Part of that decision, whether Brianna realizes it or not, is meeting Roger. That's part of what allows her to let go of her mom. I love the lines that we put in where Claire's like, 'It's not like an elevator you can just get on and off. If I leave, I might be gone from you forever. I probably will be gone for you.' So, in a way, it's like a death."

Director Brendan Maher also

> *"I think that moment is where she really puts her own feelings aside and puts her mother's first. As far as she sees it, she'll never see her mother again. It's just such a brave move. Sometimes I feel like Bree's so lonely in the world, and for her to do that was quite a big deal."*
>
> —SOPHIE SKELTON

appreciated that the episode allowed Claire to walk through everything of importance that she would be leaving behind. "Claire's learning and discovering new things all the way through this episode," he explains. "The possibility of going back is a huge concept to take on for her. In the contrast between the beats of the concepts of going back in time, there're these great human moments that are really, really lovely."

One of Maher's favorites was the opening surgical scene with Claire, which they shot on the last day of production for the episode. "It seems to be glue for the episode," he offers. "It puts Claire in the time where she's at. There was a lot of prep for that scene. We had medical advisers in. We set up the operation. We got real nurses to use in the background. And Caitriona had to come in and learn to operate on someone. She had to learn how to use a scalpel, all the body parts, and what they did and how to re-

move them. It was a logistics nightmare, but she was just so patient rehearsing all that stuff, wanting to get it right. Once that went down, she could start telling the story of the scene. We did a lot of coverage on this scene, because they were so good at it, I didn't want to lose anything that they had done and prepped for. And we had this fantastic body prosthetic that could breathe."

Graphia was happy that the episode became more emotional as it evolved, and she was especially grateful that the Christmas setting, which was a last-minute addition in her scripting, was allowed. "There was some emotionality that I wanted to go a level deeper, and I kept thinking, *What can I do to just give this a little more resonance?*" she remembers. "Then somehow it hit

me: *Oh, if it was Christmas, it would make sense that Roger's coming for the holidays, not just popping in.* And this was his first Christmas without his father."

With the idea coming a mere week before shooting, Graphia immediately called Matt Roberts in Scotland to ask if it was possible.

"He was like, 'Holy smokes!'" she laughs. "But a couple days later, he called me back. I picked up the phone and he said, 'It's beginning to look a lot like Christmas.' I let out a scream because I was so happy and thanked him for making that happen. I knew that it was a herculean task on the part of the whole crew."

The intimacy of their gift exchange and then goodbyes also gave Balfe a quiet showcase for Claire's maternal strength and heartbreak. "She's got to care for her daughter, so she's got to make it a peaceful goodbye," Maher explains. "Caitriona was right across it and is flawless again, her performance. It's really beautiful. And her sitting in the cab and her driving away, she never looked back in that scene. Even though every instinct tells her to take one last look, she never does. It's really lovely."

All of it leads to a new begin-

56

ning, as the clever puddle edit places Claire back in eighteenth-century Scotland. Graphia helped hand off the episode with Claire's POV of seeing Jamie. "I think every person online that I saw, they remembered the tinkle of the bell from the book and everyone was convinced that we were gonna have her walk up to the door, walk through it, and hear the tinkle of the bell [to end it]. We didn't want to do just the cliché cliffhanger. Matt and I decided to take it through her walking in and seeing Jamie faint because, in a way, the whole episode had been about it. In the episode, we don't see Jamie at all until the end, and we held that back because this whole episode is about getting to Jamie, and if we don't get to Jamie, it's gonna feel like a rip-off, and so we will get to the faint," she laughs.

EPISODE 306: A. MALCOLM

WRITER: MATTHEW B. ROBERTS DIRECTOR: NORMA BAILEY

Writing the reunion of Jamie and Claire from *Voyager* had long been spoken for by Matt Roberts, going all the way back to season one. "When people were thinking about 'The Wedding' and 'Faith' and all those episodes, I was thinking about *this* episode," the writer admits. "To me, of all of them, I thought that was the biggest one, so I put dibs on it."

Having had years to think about how to construct the big moment, Roberts says, the episode's Jamie-centric point of view evolved out of his desire to see Jamie's reaction to Claire walking back into his life. "I knew in episode five, in the construction of it, we were going to end it on Jamie fainting, and then you come in with 'A. Malcolm' and you start back earlier in his day. So, the idea there is, I want to see this [un-

fold]. We see what Claire's thinking about that whole time. She had time to plan what she was going to say and do. So I thought it was very important that we show that Jamie didn't plan. That's why he fainted. And I don't blame him for fainting," he chuckles. "You want that to make sense. Why would Jamie, king of men, faint? That's the reason."

Helping to realize the episode visually was veteran Canadian director Norma Bailey. She worked closely with Roberts to bring his mind's eye to the frame. "We had a lot of conversations about the approach to the reunion, because it was so significant. It was how to tease the audience, really, because everyone wanted them to just be together, like be in bed and be in love and be together," she laughs. "But the writer and producers chose to draw those moments out, so it takes a while for the actual 'reunion *reunion*' to happen."

Once Jamie and Claire enter the inner sanctum of his private room in the brothel, it essentially

> "There were a lot of [writers] who felt like Jamie would talk about his son, Willie, [to Claire] and that he would be honest about that. There was a lot of debate about that. I'll tell you, it's in the script, but I was not one of them. I felt like we could put it later in the script and it would be okay."
>
> —MATT B. ROBERTS ON A WRITERS' ROOM COMPROMISE

turns into an intimate two-person play. "There was a lot of discussion about how to approach the love scenes, because we'd seen them make love a lot in the series," Bailey says. "I suggested to Matt that I would like to slow it down, that I didn't think that ripping off your clothes was the way to go with it. So it was very important that it be done in the right way. We wanted it to definitely touch back to 'The Wedding' sequence.

"We shot in a small room for a

"I like the [breakfast] with the prostitutes; that was fun. It's lovely to do a scene like that where it's women, and women to women in a real way. Also to know the humor of it—being that Claire wasn't a prostitute but was Jamie's wife, and they were just assuming that she was one of them—was great. I loved that."

—NORMA BAILEY

"As a director, when people are going to be nude, you have to be very specific about what you're shooting so that they don't get exploited doing more than they agreed to do. So once I wrote down in detail how I wanted to shoot it, then Matt and I rehearsed with them. Not too-terrific detail, but just worked out the rhythm of it. All those things were agreed upon before we started. Then, when you're filming, little things just happen. They might say, 'Oh, I think this might work better than this way.' Those are just natural things that happen when you're shooting."

—DIRECTOR NORMA BAILEY ON THE COMPLEXITY OF SHOOTING LOVE SCENES

whole week," she continues. "That was all done chronologically because we were confined to that space anyway and it was just the two characters. They're in bed, so we wanted it to have a rhythm to it, not just the same thing all the time. They've been apart for twenty years and they're older than they

were before. She, especially, feels vulnerable about her body, because it's changed a lot. She's had a baby, and she's apprehensive that she can still be as appealing to him as she was before."

After their night of intimacy, the room ends up becoming a focal point for encounters that will deeply impact their lives going forward. "When you're confined like

"Claire comes back and Jamie's living in a brothel and there's this strange relationship with this woman who feels so comfortable that she's tying his necktie. For Claire, there's a huge amount of insecurity. I actually loved that they put in the insecurity, even of her body and being seen by Jamie again. Claire's not really been intimate with anyone, not for many years, and the last time she was intimate with him was twenty years ago. I never think of Claire as a particularly vain woman, but what person wouldn't be insecure exactly?"

—Caitriona Balfe

that, you have to find ways of being interesting," Bailey says of creatively changing up the space. "Like when she challenges him about his nephew, Young Ian—that was an interesting sequence because she finds out that [Ian's] parents don't know that [he's] there. So they start to challenge each other and they have that big argument. That was a great moment, because it was like a little cauldron in there, that space. Then she has the fight with the bad guy in there. A lot went on in that room. Confinement can sometimes force you to be creative in different ways, which is fun."

HAIR AND MAKEUP

Four seasons and fifty-five hours of narrative mean literally thousands of humans have been rendered period-accurate by *Outlander* hair and makeup designer Annie McEwan and her team. It's easy for audiences to take for granted the sheer volume of work needed to transform every actor and extra in any given scene of the series into someone who looks like they belong in another era. It's been McEwan's job since the first season to plan the overall looks for every principal actor—many of whom she helps style herself—and the background actors.

To do so, she's had to research the hair and visual trends of diverse eras, from eighteenth-century Scotland to 1960s Boston, to colonial America settlers and Native American tribes. With the help of a team of makeup artists and hairstylists that can expand in number up to forty or more, McEwan makes the denizens of the series always look camera ready.

In her thirty years of film and television work, McEwan has worked on everything from *Monarch of the Glen* to *Clash of the Titans* (2010) and even *Game of Thrones* (for which she was nominated for an Emmy Award). Her forte is non-prosthetic work, which

means all of the realistic makeup that the actors need to look authentic to the moment they're playing.

In *Outlander*'s third and fourth seasons, that means anything from Claire's sixties bouffant to Jamie's feral Dunbonnet phase. It also includes every citizen of burgeoning Wilmington, North Carolina (or at least their back-lot-built version of it), and the First Nations people representing members of the Mohawk and Cherokee tribes. It's quite the spectrum to cover, but McEwan and her artists have been up to the challenge.

After the bustle and opulence of season two's Paris settings, season three was relatively tame to prepare for, until they all relocated to South Africa, McEwan says. The challenges then came with making

the actors on the *Artemis* and the *Porpoise* ship sets look as needed, despite what may be happening in reality.

"The problem with South Africa was the wind," McEwan reveals. "They have really strong wind, and when they were becalmed in the boat for 'The Doldrums,' we couldn't have hair blowing about, creating the lie of it actually not being becalmed. So we had to stitch hair, just with a needle and thread, into the shape, so that it didn't blow about."

Other particular high points for the artists on location included re-creating the variety of Jamaican residents and natives and special guests like Geillis Duncan (Lotte Verbeek). Much as McEwan had done to age Caitriona's Claire by

twenty years, she employed the same subtle techniques for Verbeek.

"It was okay for Geillis not to change too much, because she's a witch and has all kinds of lotions and potions," McEwan explains about her overall aging. "We did put little, subtle pieces on her to try and age her, but they are subtle. And we made a wig that was a lighter shade of her red, with a little bit of gray in it."

In season four, she got to play with time again via an actor's look with Duncan Lacroix's Murtagh FitzGibbons Fraser. "The character had already aged," McEwan says of his established look in season three's "All Debts Paid." "We had to take him beyond that, as he's supposed to be about seventy [in season four]. We'd actually done the white wig for him for season three, and then the scripts changed and he wasn't in it. But we thought the wig looked so good, we'd still go with it."

Surprisingly, McEwan's favorite character arc was Roger Wakefield's transformation from a proper Oxford historian to the beaten and weathered man who meets Brianna on the grounds of River Run. "It was all about trying to make a progression of a journey that's supposed to have taken six months, when we're doing it in a matter of weeks," she details. "To try and help sell that journey was the ambition."

McEwan says they began the process at the end of season three, by having Richard Rankin try on several different hair-length wigs for the producers' review and approval. "We knew he was going to grow his hair with the boat journeys, and the producers liked the way he looks with longer hair. And Richard liked the look. Actually, he is just enthusiastic about the whole thing," she chuckles with appreciation. "He had huge makeup calls, but he never complained."

Season four also presented McEwan, and the rest of the department heads, the colossal task of re-creating two authentic Native American cultures from the ground up. "We were all really enthusiastic about the [Native Americans] because it's such a good look and such a challenge to get those big numbers made up."

As it turns out, the bigger issue became the lack of recorded reference to accurately document the tribal details of the time, McEwan says. "There're reports from travelers, and then you read another one that contradicts the one you've just read." Makeup, costumes, and production design all worked together to pin down the looks they would adopt for the Cherokee and the Mohawk.

For the makeup team, the distinctions between the tribes came down to their body art. McEwan reveals, "We gave the Mohawks the sharper tattoos, so they had right angles and more-aggressive tattoos. And the Cherokee had more organic, round tattoos with rounded shapes, to make them the softer tribe."

Creating the entire Mohawk settlement for the last two episodes of season four was an epic feat, McEwan says. An army of makeup and hair artists was brought together to transform the First Nations actors into a visually viable tribe that looked plucked out of time. "On that big day," she remembers, "including my main team, there were thirty to forty makeup and hair people. Even though it was a hundred thirty Native Americans, only one person could really fix the looks of three [people] in the big crowd shot. So we had to be on it all the time."

But the results were something special for the series, and for McEwan. "It was very time-consuming," she says in her lilting Scottish brogue. "But that pushed us, and I think that it was successful. We were very pleased with it."

EPISODE 307: CRÈME DE MENTHE

WRITER: KAREN CAMPBELL DIRECTOR: NORMA BAILEY

After the Frasers' romantic reunion, "Crème de Menthe" rolled out like a surprisingly brisk shot of reality. Season three supervising producer/writer Karen Campbell reveals that she wholeheartedly embraced exploring their life outside the reunion bubble.

"We talked about this in the room, asking, 'What does it look like when the rubber hits the road for these two?'" Campbell explains. "Because twenty years apart is not insignificant. Think of what it looks like for them to rediscover each other, not in just a romantic sense but in a sense of all their life experiences that have shaped them up to this point, because they've diverged in very specific ways.

"We know these two love each other. That's never in question," she continues. "But it's [about] seeing them have to really work at their relationship and [seeing] them have to bridge their very different points of view. Like the idea that Claire has been a surgeon and has taken an oath—Jamie can't even wrap his head around that, because her try-

"All of the crew have glutes of steel from shooting that block, because the print room is actually up a set of stairs. It's on a second floor, so anytime we had to shoot in that room, everyone had to walk up and down those stairs. Everyone was happy because our steps were up into the thousands!"

—Karen Campbell

ing to save a man who assaulted her ... It's a very black-and-white issue for him. But that vocation that

she's chosen, it's a part of who she is, and it's a principle that she can't just jettison because she happened to travel back in time. And then we really wanted to see Jamie and his bootlegging. What that looks like, and the idea that he still can't help himself with the seditious pamphlets. He still has a voice. He still very much feels that, politically, things aren't the way they should

be. So there're some ways where Jamie hasn't evolved all that much."

Figuring out how best to present those conflicts was a challenge. "When we initially broke this, we had the printshop kicking things off," Campbell explains. "Ultimately, that felt like too much of an escalation up top. The printshop burning is very memorable, so we realized that if we reverse-engineer every-

68

thing, building toward that printshop's fire, it'll give us some runway to set up important things."

The episode also introduced several plotlines that would drive the second half of the season. "It really established Young Ian's character and seeing Fergus again, and where they are in the world right now," says Campbell. "And we really wanted Jamie's lives to clash, culminating in burning down that printshop, which essentially ends his life in Edinburgh, because he's got the love of his life back."

Filming the epic fire was one of the production highlights of the season for episode director Norma Bailey and for Campbell, who was on set for the sequence. "When the printshop burns down, that all had to be figured out with storyboards, because some of it was shot in Edinburgh, some of it was shot in the back lot, and some of it was shot in the studio," Bailey reveals. "All of it had to be storyboarded so that we could literally just take the frames and say, 'This is going to be shot here, and this is going to be shot there, and this is going to be shot over there.' But *Outlander* has a

strong creative group of people that are in charge, and that makes a huge difference. They know what they're

> "We really leaned into the idea that Mr. Willoughby and Claire would have a connection because they both know what it's like to be outsiders. There's no judgment between those two, because they both know what it's like to have a different upbringing or bring a different set of skills to a table. They're able to collaborate in ways that I think other characters can't, because they know what it's like to be essentially dropped into a completely new world, a new environment with customs and different norms. Gary [Young] did such a great job with the character. He brought so much warmth and earnestness to the role."
>
> —Karen Campbell
> on Mr. Willoughby

> "With Young Ian, we were thinking about what it would be like to be that age again. He's in Edinburgh, living with his uncle, who is entrusting him with a lot of responsibility. He's one of the guys, and as one of the guys, [losing your virginity] is such a rite of passage. And particularly for Fergus, who lost his virginity in a ménage à trois. And it's interesting that it's something that Young Ian does and it's not tied to any trauma. It's tied to being that age. It's tied to having feelings of lust and having the ability to act on them because no one's here to stop you. Like any teenager. And then, yes, it was a function of us having the printshop fire be the culmination of the episode."
>
> —Karen Campbell

doing, so it's great to work with people like that."

Of Bailey, Campbell enthuses, "Norma was awesome and did wonderful work. And Matthew Roberts did an awesome job with all the second-unit printshop-burn stuff. I do recall we had many, many a meeting about that fire. The crew stepped up and just was incredible, because we only had one night in Edinburgh, shooting an exterior of a museum that's protected. We couldn't have any fire on that set, so all of those flames you saw were from the burn on the back lot on the second-unit side. And it laid over everything we shot at the actual museum right off the Royal Mile. And then the visual effects amplified the flames. Everyone just brought their A game."

EPISODE 308: FIRST WIFE

Writer: Joy Blake Director: Jennifer Getzinger

The bumpy road to the Frasers working out their new life together puts them back at Lallybroch in "First Wife." After returning Young Ian home to his parents, Claire and Jamie try to reconcile the past with their current reality. Interestingly, while many might assume bringing back Laoghaire (Nell Hudson) was what dictated the shape of this episode, in reality, the central conceit

was all about portraying Jamie and Claire's knock-down drag-out fight.

"I always look for the moment in the script that is very important, and then everything has to work around that," executive producer Matt Roberts says of that scene. "I definitely came into this from that standpoint. And then, we knew Laoghaire was going to be in the episode."

Considering the fraught past

of Claire, Jamie, and Laoghaire, the character's return to the narrative is always an emotional flash point. However, fellow executive producer Toni Graphia explains that they specifically worked to soften Laoghaire's character leading into this episode so the revelation of Jamie's marriage to her would make sense to audiences.

"We had that in mind way back in the previous season, when we did 'The Fox's Lair,' because there's no way Jamie could have married the woman that tried to get Claire killed in the witch trial," Graphia details.

"We talked about that a lot in the sense of 'Why wouldn't Claire ever tell Jamie about that?'" Roberts continues. "Saying, 'Remember Laoghaire, the girl you were making out with in the alcove when we had all that trouble? She tried to have me killed.' You'd think at some point that conversation might have taken place. We wondered if maybe it did. We conjectured. So that's why 'The Fox's Lair' is kind of the rehabilitation of Laoghaire.

"It goes back to that thing with Frank," Roberts lays out. "If they're just *so* evil and *so* despicable, there's

no dilemma for anybody. It discounts Jamie's judgment if she's that much of a horrible person. Why would Jamie ever be with her? That doesn't make a lot of sense, because it takes Jamie down a notch, and I don't like to take Jamie down a notch. I like that he's a very smart man."

Adding to the complex alchemy of producing an episode, "First Wife" was actually shot before "A. Malcolm," which forced the cast to emotionally jump ahead to play this dramatic milestone in the Frasers' relationship. "It was tricky," admits director Jennifer Getzinger. "But we

"In the book, Jamie's like, 'Oh, by the way, I was married, and I didn't tell you. And by the way, I had a son.' I mean, you can't come out with two secrets at two different times, because then Claire would be like, 'What the heck else is there?' [Jamie telling Claire about Willie immediately] was a controversial decision, but we stand by it because she was talking about Brianna, their child. It's natural that, after twenty years, Jamie would say, 'Well, I need to share this.' He shared it to be intimate and to say, 'Full disclosure, I have a son. I want you to know about it, because that's part of my life now.' But we didn't want it to hurt. So the Laoghaire thing really is its own secret in its own way."

—TONI GRAPHIA ON THE DECISION TO SPLIT JAMIE'S REVELATIONS TO CLAIRE OVER TWO EPISODES

all worked together and would remind each other where we are in the scene and how much later it is and talk about all the things that had happened between 'Surrender' and 'First Wife.' But the [writers] didn't have all those scripts yet. [The actors] were able to do it really well, but it was definitely something that would take some discussion of where we were and how we got there."

In tracking the logic of how this union even came to be, Getzinger says, "We definitely were always approaching it as this is where the story has led us and now here's Laoghaire. She didn't disappear. It's a big, shocking moment when she comes in, but in a way you do try to underplay it a little bit so that it can feel real."

Graphia adds that the portrayal of Hogmanay in Lallybroch fills in the rest of the blanks. "Jamie was missing family. He connected to Laoghaire through her daughters. He was enchanted by the young girls before he knew who their mother was, and they really filled a need for him to be a father and be the head of a family again."

And while Laoghaire goes hard on both Jamie and Claire, Getzinger has nothing but praise for Hudson's performance. "Nell is a wonderful actress," she enthuses. "I think she does a great job of bringing some heart to Laoghaire. If anything, I would say they almost cut back on how much heart she brought. In the final cut, we didn't quite show as vulnerable as Nell really went in some of the takes. It's a fine line, right? You have to find a balance between wanting to show her side of things and let her be that three-dimensional character but still protect our leads and say their connection transcends time, transcends everything."

As for the defining confrontation in the Frasers' bedroom, where Claire and Jamie physically have it out about everything, Getzinger says it's a fight that distills their frustrations into a single moment. "Here's the core cast back together. They are in this familiar setting, but yet Claire doesn't fit anymore. It's like a little bit of you can't go home

again. So you see the awkwardness and then you see the passion between them. But you also see after being apart for so many years you don't just run into each other's arms and it's all fine. It's actually really complicated and a lot has happened and there is a lot of baggage. All the love was still there, but trying to fit back into each other's lives is more difficult than either of them had thought it would be."

"We added a little bit of Claire questioning whether she should come back. In the book, Claire and Jamie are just a couple, and they're a magical couple. They don't question it once she comes back. But we added that because we thought, What happens if you leave your whole life behind in Boston, and Jamie's a criminal, and he's in trouble?

And it's not a question of whether they love each other. We didn't question that. But it was to question, 'Did I make the right decision? Maybe we had our time, instead of trying to put this together after twenty years.' We thought that made it realistic. When you see that happening on a TV screen, it might come off a little unrealistic that they never have one single doubt, because what couple doesn't? It makes them a real couple."

—Toni Graphia

SPOTLIGHT

LOTTE VERBEEK AS GEILLIS DUNCAN

When last we saw Geillis Duncan in season two, Claire, Brianna, and Roger watched the sixties-era Scottish zealot kill her husband and pass through the stones to the eighteenth century. Aware of Geillis's mission to rewrite the tragic history of Culloden, Claire knew they would cross paths back in time.

However, what Claire didn't know at the time was that Geillis would surface anew when the Frasers landed in Jamaica. Adept at reinvention, Duncan turns up on the island as a yet-again-widowed, now plantation owner on a mission to decode a prophecy that she hopes will allow her to finally course-correct Scotland's fate.

Even with her appearances being few and far between on the series, Geillis always reappears brimming with confidence and mischief as the ultimate disrupter. In keeping with that, she emerges from a pool of goat's blood in "The Bakra."

Actress Lotte Verbeek admits she was taken aback when executive producer Matt Roberts pitched that entrance, which wasn't in the original script she was sent. "The scene would have been me just talking to Ian [John Bell] and sort of interrogating him. And then [Matt] came up with the idea of placing all of that in a bloodbath, which initially I thought was a joke and laughed about. But then he said, 'I'm serious, would you do that?' Before I knew it, I said yes."

Technically, Geillis is also twenty years older than

when audiences last saw her, but she looks positively ethereal as she dramatically wipes herself clean before Young Ian in her boudoir. Verbeek expounds, "The bloodbath was a way to explain that she wouldn't have looked that old, even though she was in her fifties or sixties around that time."

The production team then augmented the actress with subtle signs of her character's true age. "I did have some facial prosthetics to make me look older, and my wig was slightly grayish and a bit more dull kind of red," she details. "And I do feel I made a point with her character to be more exhausted. She is now in a part of the world where it is hot all the time. It's humid. So I think it was more about the spirit of her being worn out a little bit."

However, Verbeek made sure to lean into Geillis's seductive side too, as that skill set has served her well in collecting so many lovers and husbands throughout time. "I think it is interesting that she has this turn-on for [Ian]," she teases. "She hasn't lost that zest, or that appetite, if you will, which I think is interesting and maybe unexpected. But, for me, it felt like it was

a mix of changes to the character that made a lot of sense."

Having played Geillis over three seasons, Verbeek says the distance between appearances did nothing to mute the character in her own mind. "Even though she gets to be quite outlandish, especially in her last season, I think the character has become really familiar to me. Going in and out of it just makes it familiar territory, so that naturally came back. And then with getting back into the accent and back into the costumes, I was there, pretty much."

Having scenes with Caitriona again in "The Bakra" and "Eye of the Storm" also brought Claire and Geillis's unique relationship full circle. As always with the pair, their commonality as time travelers infuses all of their conversations with both subtext, curiosity, and even joint admiration. "She comes to know more about Claire, so in that moment when they have this long conversation at the plantation, a lot is being revealed." Verbeek thinks that's not something Geillis has gotten to do with many, especially in her Jamaican existence. "I think in some ways she must have gotten quite alone on that island by herself. Not having friends that she's used to. I think it's always been about the cause for her."

And it's that singular cause to restore Scotland that creates another standoff with Claire, as Geillis prom-

ises to go back in time to take Brianna's life in exchange for the child she lost. "The stakes are just heightened," the actress says of the grotto scene. "And that's how things come to an end. They are the final moments between the two characters, and ultimately Claire acts out of self-defense, or defense, of her daughter. I don't know that Claire ever really intended to kill Geillis, but when she does, it's too late. So it's quite dramatic."

EPISODE 309: THE DOLDRUMS

WRITER: SHANNON GOSS DIRECTOR: DAVID MOORE

Determined to retrieve Young Ian from the pirates who kidnapped him, Jamie and Claire start "The Doldrums" by securing passage on Captain Raines's *Artemis* to Jamaica. In the West Indies they hope to find the ship that spirited him away. With the Frasers now in motion again, co-executive producer Luke Schelhaas says the writers' room debated if their sea-travel

> *"I have to say, with the two boats, it's amazing how good the visual effects are, because there was not a drop of water near those boats. To see all that at sea, and the boats sailing along, it's incredible. It really pulls the whole story together."*
>
> —DIRECTOR DAVID MOORE

story should be limited to just one episode but then decided it should span two.

"There was everything that led up to the end of 'The Doldrums,' which is Claire being taken aboard the *Porpoise* to deal with the epidemic outbreak and being, essentially, kidnapped," he details. "And then, thereafter, that was a nice, clean break for an episode leading up to the moment that she jumps

off the *Porpoise*. We also knew that we had a great character in Captain Raines [Richard Dillane]. So one thing that we began to lean into was this idea of the superstitions that these sailors had. We did a lot of research into these seafaring superstitions and this idea of the law of the sea."

British director David Moore joined the series for the first time to steer the voyage episodes, which were the first to be shot in South Africa. "It was a big adventure, the first episodes I did," Moore enthuses. "They were set on these

amazing sailing ships that are docked at Cape Town Studios."

He continues, "We had to work out technically how to go about making these episodes feel like they were happening at sea. Those boats in Cape Town don't go anywhere. They exist in the car park, so you're essentially working within a greenscreen world, putting on the sea effects afterward. But you're able to blow water at the boats and fill the sails with wind using big fans. That took a long time, storyboarding and setting all that up."

Inside the ship, there was plenty

of drama to stage too, as Jamie, Claire, Mr. Willoughby, Fergus, and his stowaway handfasted wife, Marsali, have to navigate the close quarters. "That moment that Jamie realizes Fergus has sneaked Marsali aboard, the way Sam, Caitriona, César, and everyone played that was really great," Schelhaas chuckles. "It gives you tension for the episode. It gives you plot, and it gives you plot for the next episode, but also a nice comic moment of lightness to start off that episode."

Sorting out their sleeping arrangements below decks gave Moore

the opportunity to embrace the claustrophobia. "It's a bit like doing a submarine movie: You want to give a feeling of what it's like to live in these confined spaces without battering your head off a wooden beam, and we did that with amazing regularity," he laughs.

Schelhaas says the scenes between Claire and Marsali in particular were perfectly suited to that scenario. "Marsali certainly doesn't let it lie, how she feels about Claire," he says, smiling. "You put those two in cramped quarters, force them together, and force them to work out some of their differences over the course of this episode. It was a lot

> "[Gary Young] did an amazing job, because that speech is something like five pages long. He learned it in its entirety. A scene that goes that long is tricky in the sense that it's very difficult for everybody to keep the tension through for so long, but everybody bought into it. We shot it from like twelve different camera positions, both for him, the storyteller, and then the various characters in the background. So that was, in a way, like a little play. It had a really nice flow to it."
>
> —DIRECTOR DAVID MOORE ON MR. WILLOUGHBY'S SPEECH

of fun and we knew we had some rich material there for these great actresses. It's not easy for either one of those characters to forget about that shared history they have."

However, it was a scene back on the main deck that Moore counts as his favorite. "It's the big scene where they're caught in the doldrums and the crew believe that

there's a Jonah on board, and the finger gets pointed at Hayes [James Allenby-Kirk]. There's a whole action sequence, which involved putting people on wires and climbing up the rigging to rescue the Jonah. And then Mr. Willoughby comes to the rescue and tries to avert their attention by telling his life story. That was a huge scene, which took a lot of planning with stunt people and the building of various bits of set. We built a scale set of rigging down near the ground with safety mats. That took us about three or four days to shoot that one sequence. So that was a big, quite exciting undertaking."

"The [audience] knows what Caitriona looks like really. They've had three seasons of seeing her face. [Adding age makeup] would just beggar belief, and they would question it, so we're never going to do that. The fact that her hair is now a very simple hairstyle, tied back, adds to [her older look]. And costumes dressed her down. She hasn't got the fancy dresses, so you see less flesh on her. I think that helps sell [her age]. Also, Cait is really a good actress. She brings gravitas. She brings the age of her character to her character. She's changed her character and the way she performs. With all these things, the actor has to bring it, and she brings it. I believe whatever she's trying to sell me, really."

—MAKEUP AND HAIR DESIGNER ANNIE MCEWAN ON NOT OVERDOING CAITRIONA'S AGE MAKEUP

EPISODE 310: HEAVEN AND EARTH

WRITER: LUKE SCHELHAAS ✦ DIRECTOR: DAVID MOORE

Jamie and Claire are separated once more as the *Porpoise* sails away from the *Artemis* in "Heaven and Earth." When Jamie protests, he's confined in the bulkhead by Captain Raines. Meanwhile, as the conscripted ship surgeon on the British man-of-war, Claire is consumed with containing the typhoid-fever outbreak.

As the assigned writer, co–executive producer Luke Schelhaas admits he was excited to tackle the emotional story of the infected *Porpoise* crew. "I thought there was a lot of rich material there. There's some action and some adventure certainly, but what I responded to, and what I was really happy came through in the script, was the rela-

tionship between Claire and Elias Pound [Albie Marber]. That was the heart of the episode, and I fell in love with all of that."

While Pound is an essential character in the book, Schelhaas says they decided to make him the emotional spine of the entire episode. "He brings out something new in Claire," the writer explains. "There's a protectionism there. It was shocking that you would see boys as young as seven, let alone fourteen, on these ships. So when the captain says, 'I'll put my best man at your side to help you with this,' and it's a fourteen-year-old

> *"There's a scene early on where Elias gives Claire a hat on the deck and he says the sun can get awfully hot. I think it's a really sweet, subtle moment; I just love the way he played it. I loved her reaction because she's just been stern with him down below and she sees that he's not shying away from her. He's going to be a helpful assistant. He's wiser than his years."*
>
> —Luke Schelhaas on Elias Pound

boy?" he asks with incredulity. "For Claire to experience the shock of that, of what this time was, not only in the disease outbreak but all of these details, was really fun to play. Adjusting to the time she's done before, but here's something she's *never* done before.

"Also, she's just left her daughter back home," Schelhaas continues. "I think she's thinking about Brianna. And here's a young kid, a different age, but it's a mother–son relationship that develops there. She doesn't have Jamie, so she needs someone to confide in, and it's this young kid."

> "The scene wasn't specifically in the book, but you take little clues and you make something of them, so where Elias says, 'How do you remain so calm in the face of death?' she then says, 'Compartmentalizing,' which is something she learned to do as a doctor and is something she does every day since. But she can't do it when it comes to Elias and when he dies. For us, that was a great thing to lead an episode toward."
>
> —LUKE SCHELHAAS

> "With the ships, we tried to make a difference between the crew on the Porpoise and the crew on the Artemis, in that the Navy guys had tied-back hair, and the guys in Jamie's ship, we tried to keep their hair loose. So if there was a quick cut from one to the other, the audience would be able to know what ship they were on."
>
> —HAIR AND MAKEUP DESIGNER ANNIE McEWAN

Creating a unique environment on this ship was the focus of returning director David Moore, who wanted to diversify the look and feel of the second of his two ship-based episodes. "You always try and get a sense of the detail of what it would be like in terms of working as a doctor and what could be demonstrative to push the idea of this plague-ridden ship and what all of that meant for everybody," he explains. "We wanted to make it as dank and dark and smelly as ever possible to have [Smell-O-Vision] on TV. Then, when she sets to work and gets all the people around to

organize, she throws up the hatches and slogs down the decks. You get a sense of that mess being cleared away and lightness invading the bowels of the ship again."

For the mass funeral on the deck, they strove for accuracy in how to portray it. "We spent a lot of time looking at records and reading historical references to try and get the procedure right, as much as possible," Moore details. "Shooting that big funeral was another big set. People describe it as an emotional one, even when what you're throwing over the side is a whole bunch of dummies sewn into canvas. But it has that real feeling,

"At the end, Claire decides she's going to jump overboard, and the wonderful Swedish milkmaid talks her into giving it a go. That was quite crazy and fun. The crazy part was the time, because Claire had to take quite a lot of her clothes off so that she wouldn't sink. Trying to get all that eighteenth-century cover off was quite a number, and we had to cheat that in many ways and then package it all up in her bundle and then get her to leap over."

—Director David Moore

and we wanted that concentrated emotion within that for both Claire and for Elias, whose friend back home had died in front of his very eyes."

By the last act of the episode, Claire manages to turn the tide of the outbreak, but there is an awful price when Pound comes down with the fever and she can't save him. "When Claire puts that rabbit foot back to be buried with him at sea, then for the sailmaker to hand her the needle and say, 'It must be done by a friend,' I think that is my favorite moment. Caitriona is *so* good in that; she just breaks your heart."

SPOTLIGHT

DAVID BERRY AS LORD JOHN GREY

While Claire and Jamie are the beating heart of the *Outlander*-verse, there's another character who is just as near and dear to the heart of its creator, Diana Gabaldon: Lord John William Grey. He's featured in seven of Gabaldon's *Outlander* books and is the central character in nine separate novels or novellas.

Beloved by the book fans, John is introduced to the series fans in season two's "Je Suis Prest." Claire and Jamie manipulate the young British boy into giving them important information affecting the outcome of the Battle of Prestonpans. But the character really gets his due in season three, when we meet Lord John as an adult in "All Debts Paid," now played by Australian actor David Berry.

Known in his home country for television work in *Home and Away* and his long-running role as James Bligh in *A Place to Call Home*, Berry was approached in 2016 to audition for *Outlander* on tape. "I remember the audition was probably the next day, and I wasn't

gung-ho about having to learn ten pages of dialogue that had been sent to me, as I'm a bit lazy," Berry laughs lightly. A new parent at the time too, Berry says he made the time to read the script and was impressed. "I decided that I'd just go in and wing it, because it's the first audition I had in quite some time after being available."

Berry chuckles as he remembers going in to audition with a friend from driving school, who was "doing the worst Scottish accent.

"I feel like it was more an art piece than an audition," he jokes. "But for whatever reason, they responded to it and then it was very quick. I found myself on set within a week, not knowing much at all of what the show is about or anything aside from the ten pages that I had been given. Winging it was the strategy I adopted first, and it worked okay."

Berry says he used the quick turnaround to inform how he played Grey's entry into the story. "The whole way I got the job, and the way I was thrust into it, is not

too dissimilar from the way Lord John is thrust into his own adventures. He's a bit on the back foot, not knowing where he is, and is treading water, trying to piece it all together. And that's certainly what David was going through, so it definitely did inform my character."

When he received a character outline and scripts, Berry sought inspiration by watching certain films that featured performances he wanted to pull from. "I was watching *Lawrence of Arabia*, then a lot of films with Errol Flynn, from his thirties films. [Actor] Jonathan Pryce's stuff. And *The Princess Bride*. It was sort of that amalgam of the English gentleman. Swashbucklers are not something that is natural to me. I'm Australian, but I felt like I had to get in that mindset."

He, of course, also leaned on the series itself, watching his first episodes on his flight over to Scotland for his first days of production. "I admired Sam's work immensely," the actor enthuses. "The work he'd done from seasons one and two was really great. And then Sam was very, very generous and welcoming, to my surprise," he laughs cheekily. "I think I was anticipating that he'd probably be some big shot and wouldn't have time for me. But he did a *Welcome to the cast!* tweet. That he even had time to write that, that's such a lovely thing. It only engendered in me even more admiration for the guy."

Berry's debut episode, "All Debts Paid," featured several scenes of Grey and Jamie, first sizing each other up and then forming a genuine friendship. To sell the authenticity of that arc, Berry admits, "Maybe I was a bit nervous, but I thought it was quite useful to keep a distance from [Sam]. I wanted those moments of meeting each other to feel very fresh with feeling each other out. So we didn't know much of each other, and I think the less that we talked about it and the more distance I kept from him in those early stages was useful for the relationship. Of course, we got to know each other more and more," he quickly adds. "We became more friends, but just in terms of the work, that was the strategy I employed."

And then there was the dawning realization for Berry about just how popular Lord John was with the *Outlander* book fandom. "That was one of the most intimidating things about getting the job," he says, a bit exasperated. "The character was *so* well liked, and not only that, he had copious amounts of things written about him. I'm an actor who likes to do his research and know what I'm doing, and to just go in blindly—winging it—was a very anxious place for me to be. I really had no choice. The time frame was such that I had to double down on my own instincts and just go with what I had time to learn in the script."

The actor got only two episodes to get comfortable in Grey's skin, and then the character was out of the narrative until the last two episodes of season three. "I remember at one stage, there was going to be more Lord John in Jamaica and I was going to go to South Africa," he reveals. "But for reasons unknown to me, they filmed all my stuff as interiors [in Scotland], so I didn't have to go to South Africa. I filmed all my stuff in Edinburgh at the end."

Berry was then back for four episodes of season four, when Lord John Grey and his adopted son, Willie, relocate to Virginia. He received the script for "Blood of My Blood" well in advance and says he emailed director Denise Di Novi and the producers some thoughts he had on the emotional scenes between Grey and Claire.

"The director of the episode was so lovely and accommodating and took on everything that I had to say," he praises. "Those were the strongest memories I take away from that episode, that she was just nurturing. Denise's passion for this character really came through and guided us through the difficulties we had."

Playing two people coming to reconcile their love for Jamie Fraser was a complicated dance for the two actors, but Berry is very pleased with the end result and getting some one-on-one scenes with Caitriona. "I was really looking forward to having more to do with her in season three, so then having those scenes in the cabin was a good consolation for the things that were left out in season three. The whole episode is just so nicely constructed for Lord John, and it just gives the audience the opportunity to really dig into his vulnerabilities and get to know him on a deeper level."

As Claire tends to John's measles, the Fraser cabin becomes an intimate confessional for the two, and Berry says his character eventually leaves changed. "I think it empowers John," he contends. "I don't think one exchange is going to completely turn the character around, but it's definitely a step forward for him. I think the gift that she gives him is the gift of acceptance and the permissiveness to be who he is. He's never heard from anyone of his time that it's okay to be who he is. She says he deserves happiness, and I don't think he's ever really taken on, in a meaningful way, that he deserves happiness. That is his cross to bear, that he will never be happy. But she says, 'No, he deserves happiness.' What that means then is he goes on his journey to find his happiness."

But first he has to help another Fraser—Brianna, in "If Not For Hope." Berry thinks John heeds the call due to friendship, and "maybe there's a fascination to see who Brianna is, but I don't really think that's his primary motivator. I think by default he's a very compassionate man. I think that the experiences that he's gone through in his life have given him an insight into the world that necessitates him sympathizing with the plight of someone in distress or under oppression or not being able to live happily."

With seven hours of Lord John Grey adventures now under Berry's belt, the character is coming to him more easily now. "I come in and out of [the series], but I definitely do feel that through the opportunities I've been given, I got to know his soul a bit better," the actor says. "I definitely feel more confident that I know the man, and we know the man, a lot better. Even if Lord John does the craziest things in the future, we still have a whole body of work, and of life, that he's portrayed onscreen that really goes into showing who this man is . . . at least as best as I could play him."

EPISODE 311: UNCHARTED

WRITERS: KAREN CAMPBELL AND SHANNON GOSS

DIRECTOR: CHARLOTTE BRÄNDSTRÖM

One of the most unconventional episodes of the season, "Uncharted" follows—without dialogue for the first twenty minutes—the aftermath of Claire's jump into the ocean and her subsequent days in the jungle looking for food, water, and rescue.

The episode was jointly written by Karen Campbell and Shannon Goss, and was initially split in half, Campbell explains, with her writing the opening half and Goss writing the back half.

"We really liked the idea of seeing Claire in survival mode," Campbell says of the episode's heart. "She

has a wealth of knowledge when it comes to survival, growing up with Uncle Lamb, who brought her along on archaeology digs. She's very much a tomboy, so we really embraced the idea of seeing what Claire would do to survive. She does know how to start a fire. She does know where to look for water."

Internationally renowned director Charlotte Brändström was tasked with bringing this episode to life, and she paid special care to finding locations in South Africa for Claire's solitary trek. "We really came to find the right venues to tell the story, to see her journey, and make it as difficult as possible," she explains. "One of the beaches needed to be the beach where she washed up. We needed it to look like a really isolated island, and the other part was the beach where [the *Artemis*] wrecked."

To open the episode with more stakes, Brändström added the scene where Claire first falls off the log into the ocean and then washes up on the beach. "You're trying to make it as cinematic, as interesting, and as exciting as possible when you come in," the director details.

"The episode was very visual and it was wonderful to be out in nature, but it was tough because it was a lot of hiking and walking and we were trying very hard to get the right light."

She continues, "I remember the day we were on the beach, Caitriona was really sick, but she just

"We were really having to get under the skin of what exactly you would do if you were marooned on a desert island. Claire took her skirt off and wrapped it round her head. Her skirt came off, got ripped in half to bandage her legs when she was bitten by the ants. The costume was solving a lot of the drama and was really telling the story."
—ASSISTANT COSTUME DESIGNER NINA AYRES ON THE LAST OF THE "BAT SUIT"

kept shooting. She's amazing like that. She didn't care that she was sweating. She didn't care what she looked like. The makeup artist was great, because we made her dirty, we made her sweaty; she had to have all these big bites on her legs from the ants. It was really important that she didn't look beautiful. There was nothing glamorous about it. She just needed to look

fierce. The fact that she was able to make it so interesting is why I find it a very strong episode."

Claire survives her desperate hike and is found by the slightly mad Father Fogden. "He really popped in the source material," Campbell says of the character. "So we tried to find a way to still incorporate him and have him be a cautionary tale of what could happen to Claire if she doesn't find Jamie. He's this heartbroken man who lost the love of his life and now self-medicates."

"In the [book], there was a pirate fight on the ship, and that's how Claire wound up getting her arm cut open. We immediately knew that we would never be able to do that. However, Shannon and I were thinking, Wouldn't it be cool, when Claire is escaping Fogden, if there was a pirate who had seen her, and he followed her to wherever she was going. And [while he's] following her, she finds Jamie. The ship has not been fully repaired, so it's still on the beach. The pirate follows Claire, sees this ship, tells his pirate buddies, and then we have a huge beach battle between Jamie and the *Artemis* crew. *It was gonna be awesome. Everyone was gonna have big hero moments. We were super psyched and then production came back to us, and bless their hearts, said, 'This is* way *too big.'"*

—KAREN CAMPBELL ON THE SCENE THAT WAS CUT

"It's not that easy to make something believable when you speak to a coconut," Brändström continues with a laugh. "Nick Fletcher is a very strong actor, so when his name came up, I knew to jump on it because I felt that he was really the right person. The producers and the writers all loved him. He has the humor, he's smart, and it seems that he's high on whatever he was smoking, so he made it real."

In the last act, Claire and Jamie dramatically reunite on the beach in a peak romantic moment for the

pair and the series. They were on location at the time, and Campbell effuses, "There was magic the day that we shot that. I even think there were dolphins playing in the surf. The aesthetics of it were stunning and beautiful, and it captured that *From Here to Eternity* epic romantic vibe. The take we wound up using was the one that, even on the day, I was like, 'Oh, that's the *one*.' Not only were the actors really wonderful, but our Steadicam operator, Michael Carstensen, was money that day. He has to run as fast as Sam, carrying an over-fifty-pound camera rig, and stop at the right moment when they stop and collide. It's very tricky and very technical, but he nailed it. So, in that instance, I think it was better than even what Shan and I originally envisioned."

Then, back on the *Artemis*, fans got the follow-up treat of tipsy

Claire and Jamie's moment of passion, which is a fan favorite from the book. Brändström and the producers knew there would be huge expectations around it, so she was given a full day to shoot it. "The actors really gave one hundred percent," she says. "They had an afternoon of rehearsal, so it was very rehearsed when we came in,

and we still found different things. Like the moment when Caitriona starts crawling on the table, that was not rehearsed. That was her coming up with it."

"That huge snake in the jungle I showed to the office, so Caitriona had to come meet it. The snake was actually crawling around the conference room. Caitriona knew she had to play with it, so she just held it like everything was fine. She held it in her arms and said, 'This is gonna be great.' Later [on set], the snake was supposed to crawl over her, but then the snake, I think, got very comfortable and it just [lay] there. But once the snake was off, she just jumped up in the air and was so happy to be rid of it."

—DIRECTOR CHARLOTTE
BRÄNDSTRÖM

EPISODE 312: THE BAKRA

WRITER: LUKE SCHELHAAS DIRECTOR: CHARLOTTE BRÄNDSTRÖM

"The Bakra" sets up a confluence of characters who will stoke the incendiary events making up the final two hours of the season. Co–executive producer Luke Schelhaas was responsible for putting all of the players on the proverbial chessboard as they reveal themselves in Jamaica.

First, Young Ian is introduced back into the story as the episode

> "When Lord John Grey gets his reading, as [Margaret's] holding that sapphire of his, he stands up and says, 'What a peculiar pastime.' When I saw that for the first time, I didn't write the line, and I cracked up."
>
> —LUKE SCHELHAAS

opens with him. "There's this whole bit of the book that you don't see

much of what happens to Young Ian once he's kidnapped by the pirates aboard the *Bruja*," Schelhaas explains. "He talks about it with Jamie, after he's rescued. We actually used some of that [dialogue] in the fourth season, but for the story that he tells here, we decided to put that on camera. Not so much his trip across the ocean but his kidnapping and then what happened to him once he was there on the island."

That sets up the visually stunning reveal of Geillis Duncan as the owner of the *Bruja*. It's a true jaw-dropper as she erotically emerges from a pool of blood, first baring just her leg and then her whole self to a bewildered Young Ian.

"That was exciting, to bring Geillis back," Schelhaas admits with a smile. "Interestingly, initially we spread [her] scenes throughout the episode. But we decided in post-production that we really ought to play all of those scenes up front. It was partly inspired by how we wanted to introduce Geillis in the episode. We realized we wanted our first shot of Geillis to be that moment where the leg comes out of the bloodbath. In the script, there was a scene prior to that where the pirates come and bring her the jewels and say, 'We've got a boy for you.' We decided as great as that scene was, that can't be the introduction

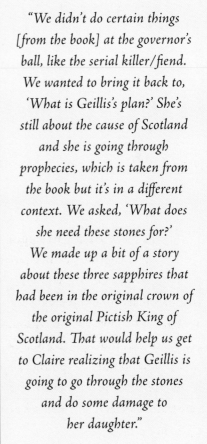

"We didn't do certain things [from the book] at the governor's ball, like the serial killer/fiend. We wanted to bring it back to, 'What is Geillis's plan?' She's still about the cause of Scotland and she is going through prophecies, which is taken from the book but it's in a different context. We asked, 'What does she need these stones for?' We made up a bit of a story about these three sapphires that had been in the original crown of the original Pictish King of Scotland. That would help us get to Claire realizing that Geillis is going to go through the stones and do some damage to her daughter."

—LUKE SCHELHAAS

to Geillis when you have *that* moment of her rising out of the bloodbath."

As with most impressive shots, this one took a tremendous amount of work to pull off. Director Charlotte Brändström concedes it took a lot of trial and error to get Geillis's introduction just right. "It took a whole day to shoot that, but it was a great set. The production design was wonderful, and it was something I had never seen before. She starts with her leg up in the air, and it reminded me of the posters for this old movie with Dustin Hoffman called *The Graduate*.

"First, the blood was very slippery, so once she got out of the bloodbath, it was very hard for [Lotte] not to slip, because it was oily. Then, as [Lotte] was just lying in that bath, we made sure it was the right temperature and covered her completely with blood, because

"There was a lot to that scene because fake blood is quite slippery, so we had to make the tiles a little more rugged. I was wearing sticky Band-Aids under my feet so I would not slip and slide, to make it look a bit more sexy than that. My greatest effort was to not fall flat on my face. We rehearsed that scene before we shot it. We took about half a day for all the departments to see what was going to happen and how to prepare. They made that quite an important moment. A lot of time was invested into that to make everybody comfortable and to make it look the way it ultimately did. I loved my scenes with John Bell. He was a great actor to work with, so that to me was a highlight."

—LOTTE VERBEEK

time," Schelhaas continues. "The confrontation between the two of them, though largely taken from the book, is in a very different setting. But that moment where Claire sees her across the room and says, 'I think I've seen a ghost,' and leaves John Grey to have that conversation was fantastic.

she had to be naked. And then she had to jump on this young boy, and that was also quite something," she laughs.

After that sequence, the story then refocuses on the Frasers in this new country that treats slavery as commerce. In a particularly disturbing sequence, Claire is witness to a slave auction. Brändström says, "The auction was actually very tough for me emotionally, but it's part of history, and it's very accurate. It all has to be real, it all has to make sense, and there was a load of research done with everything in the details."

The narrative then culminates in the governor's ball, which hosts a cross section of the populace and puts all of the main players under the same roof. "It was really fun to play the sideshow at the governor's ball," Schelhaas notes. "[The Campbells] are doing readings for the crowd, and then the governor

himself, Lord John Grey, gets involved. Playing the John Grey and Jamie reunion at the governor's ball was a lot of fun, as was playing Claire meeting John Grey [again]. She reads him very quickly, that he's got some feelings for [her] husband.

"But I think the thing that that episode aims toward, and builds toward all along, is the moment that Claire sees Geillis for the first

> "The gown when Geillis gets out of the bloodbath, that was a fabric that I sourced [in South Africa]. It was like an upholstery linen. She's trying to seduce [Ian] and know more about his history. The choice of that garment wasn't a very eighteenth-century-looking choice. I don't know what other time periods she's traveled to, but it didn't have to be eighteenth century with her."
>
> —Assistant Costume
> Designer Nina Ayres

TOT313_023_030_v020

BUILDING SEASON THREE: VISUAL EFFECTS

Outlander isn't the first series that comes to mind when someone lists a visual-effects-heavy series. In fact, the show had been able to lean on practical production techniques for the most part until they started production on season three. "They were more of what we call 'cleaning up' things," executive producer Matt Roberts explains about how they typically used "VFX" (visual effects).

Because *Outlander* is a period drama, VFX work was primarily focused on subtracting contemporary things, like electrical lines, new buildings, or even planes in the sky, out of a shot frame. But as the show got more ambitious with its locales and dramatic sequences, visual-effects supervisor Richard Briscoe was called in more and more to make onscreen digital magic. Here he shares the inside story behind some of his favorite scenes:

01:02:59:09

Woodridge Productions Inc.
TOTT301_LC2_V
BALANCE/ADD SMOKE, BODIES EXTENSIONS, SPEED FX 200%

⚛ The Battle of Culloden

We talked about [the battle] a lot. The first exploration was, really, how do we tell the story? Stylistically and financially, we don't want to do *The Lord of the Rings* or *Game of Thrones*. Instead, it was all about how Jamie experienced that environment, rather than him on top of the hill with the generals watching it all.

During the production, even with two hundred combatants, you very quickly run out of people as the camera moves around. So the majority of the work for us was [putting] in additional combatants. And then it was about safety and things that you couldn't do on the day with cast right there. We added explosions and some cannonball hits. We added more fire and a lot more ash and cinders in the air, so it was an enhancement gig rather than self-conscious visual effects.

⚛ Claire's Arrival in Edinburgh

Claire's arrival was set in the Royal Mile, which is a famous street in Edinburgh. But it's a major, major street. There's no way you can shut it down for filming. Plus, there is too much modernity. So that whole scene was basically shot in a car park at the back of the studio, in a green-screen corridor. We rebuilt the Royal Mile around them and laid a section of cobbled street about eighty foot long and did all of the scenes in that [area]. With VFX, we extended it and put in the buildings on either side, which was a 3-D process. We built them in 3-D from site surveys and extensive photographs of the real place and we ended up using a virtual camera

01:50:50:19

Woodridge Productions Inc.
6_030_RYM - GREEN-SCREEN SET EXTENSION

system. By the time we filmed, we had a rough version of our model, so from the screen as we filmed, we could frame up and see what buildings would be in our shot and how to frame relative to them.

The Burning of A. Malcolm's Printshop

The exterior of the printshop was a real location in Edinburgh, which was a historical building and a museum. We couldn't even shoot inside the door, let alone set fire to it. So we shot that as if it was on fire. We had some flames on stands out-

side just to give [the exterior] some appropriate lighting.

Then we built a facsimile of the building, just in terms of its rough shape and size, into what we call a black box. We could then burn it and superimpose the two [shots]. The superimposition took a lot of lining up cameras and matching angles. And because it was a controlled burn, special effects could stop and start, and we could go stage by stage instead of just setting fire to it and hoping we got [the footage].

For the inside of the printshop, it was a bit like the battlefield in

that there was only an amount of fire we could do for real inside, because I had crew in there. The inside was a set on the stage, and things will catch for real very quickly. We ended up adding [digital] fire and smoke to create that inferno.

Sailing to Jamaica

We started prep for [them sailing for Jamaica] right at the beginning of season three. For the external shots, we'd have to have digital versions of those ships. And for the on-set scenes on the deck, we'd have shots of digital water, which is generally simulated.

Black Sails shot in South Africa, so along with their ships, we took over their digital ship models and revamped them by moving the sails around. We still had a lot to do, but we didn't have to start from scratch on the ships.

We went to VFX [companies] with experience making digital water. And I should also say that some of the more-pedestrian sequences—of, say, Claire on the *Porpoise* sailing along—some of that was just plates [or footage without actors] of seawater that we'd shot and put in the background. But that only works for certain angles or where the camera isn't moving around much. As soon as you've got quite dynamic camera movement, you really have to do a 3-D ocean.

TOT313_023_030_SIM_v019
tt023030_anim_pirates_v033

⚓ Eye of the Storm

For the storm sequence at the end of the season, just with the timescale, we had to split [the sequence] across two VFX companies. Logistically, there was no other way. But then you have another level of continuity to balance. You've got to make the two [companies] realize each other's continuity as well.

All of those shots, just in terms of computer processing, take a lot of time. And then with the edit, you're making sure this wave's coming up here at this point, so in the reverse shot, it needs to be going down. Plus, while we might move the camera around the ship, the ship itself isn't moving, so we have to create the impression that it's pitching and rolling by moving the water and moving the horizon. That again becomes a choreography of the water coming up, or the horizon coming up, which tells us the bow is going down. When we reverse it, we need to go the other way. We had

Sam and Caitriona in the storm doing the *Star Trek* kind of acting, pretending the ship is pitching and rolling. You then have to time and work your horizon to their movement. That is a lot of work, and it took a lot of effort from a big team of probably sixty people.

In 2018, "Eye of the Storm" was nominated for two Visual Effects Society Awards: Outstanding Supporting Visual Effects in a Photoreal Episode, and Outstanding Effects Simulations in an Episode, Commercial, or Real-Time Project (for the Stormy Seas).

ADR SAILORS - TBW

St. John the Baptist Parish Library
2920 New Hwy. 51
LaPlace, LA 70068

EPISODE 313: EYE OF THE STORM

WRITERS: TONI GRAPHIA AND MATTHEW B. ROBERTS

DIRECTOR: MATTHEW B. ROBERTS

As at the end of season two, Toni Graphia and Matt Roberts were tasked with the huge responsibility of writing *Outlander's* third-season finale. But unlike in season two, it was decided that Roberts would direct too.

That wasn't a big leap, because since season one, Roberts had

> *"The scenes with Claire and Geillis and Jamie going through their meeting in the cave, all that was filmed at a separate time [when Lotte was on set]."*
>
> —MATT ROBERTS ON THE SCENE HE DIDN'T SHOOT FOR THE FINALE

been responsible for shooting the title-card sequences and directing second-unit teams to get insert shots, extra footage, or do needed reshoots.

"The first two seasons we called second unit the 'MRU,' which is the Matt Roberts Unit," he jokes. "We would do so many big [scenes],

like when we were double-banking, or when you're filming main unit in one spot and you're filming another main unit in another spot. Because 'Eye of the Storm' was the thirteenth episode, it was also the one block that had one episode. We were in South Africa as well, and that is a long journey for any director to make. But I was able to prep [the episode] at the same time as covering the other blocks, and having co-written that episode as well, then I could do the rewrites there.

"Plus, I shot the storm sequence anyway, and that's a huge sequence in the episode," he continues. "We shot that first, almost right when we got to South Africa, because we knew we needed so much time with the visual effects. So in talking with Ron, and Starz, and Sony, everybody signed off on it."

As for the scripting, both Roberts and Graphia admit it was a

> "The behind-the-scenes of [the storm sequence] is absolutely amazing. You step up onto a real ship, and we tilt it over, and a huge tank of water dumps over and knocks Sam down, and he's lovin' it. Both Sam and Cait really got into that and gave it their all, and I think it shows."
>
> —MATT ROBERTS

packed episode to fit everything into in just one hour. "People kept saying, 'How are you going to fit all that in? The end of that book is crazy,'" Graphia laughs. "But it was the most relaxed writing that I've done. We always knew we were going to start with Claire floating

"We have had conversations
with the producers where they
said, 'Well, you never know'
[about Geillis returning], with
that knowing look. We'll see.
Never say never. We don't know
what the future, or the past,
holds for Geillis. It's time travel,
so everything is possible."

—LOTTE VERBEEK

"The outfit that Geillis
gets beheaded in was a sixties
cape. It was more for where she
was heading to, as it was
obviously quite unusual for the
eighteenth century. But it doesn't
matter what she wears, as
she's mad anyway. There was
always that thought in my head,
that it didn't have to adhere to
the rules that everybody else
adheres to, apart from people
that do time travel."

—ASSISTANT COSTUME
DESIGNER NINA AYRES

and do the 'I was dead' [monologue] as the opening and then catch up to it. I love that, because I love seeing that image. It's very surreal. And then that episode has three segments, which is the Geillis and Claire cat-and-mouse game, then the voodoo section, and then the ocean section. We both just picked our favorite things, and then we'd trade them back and forth, and then we'd both rewrite each other. And knowing that he was directing it, it's kind of director-proof."

Roberts adds, "The season-three finale was much more plot-driven. We had to finish stories and they had much bigger set pieces. It had all the elements of the Caribbean. We had the ships, it was in the jungle, and there were caves, so we had all these elements to mesh together to finish off the story. We probably could have used another hour to do that. I would have loved to do another hour to finish off the season, because, for me, it felt a little compacted in the storytelling of it all. And that's just because we had so much to do and so little time. I think if it was a different director, who didn't know *Outlander* and

> *"When I was editing the finale and going over*
> *the music cues, I asked Bear [McCreary] if he*
> *would put in pipes and drums over the credits.*
> *He liked the idea. I thought that would lead us to*
> Drums of Autumn. *That was an idea that I had early*
> *on in the script, but I didn't put it actually*
> *in the script, so I just asked Bear and he,*
> *of course, did a great job."*
>
> —Matt Roberts

how we did things, it would have been much more difficult."

Regardless of the challenges, Roberts was pleased and proud of the final results. He especially remembers the last scene of the season, which was the beach scene after Claire and Jamie surface from the storm. "When we were filming the beach scenes, there was an actual storm swell out to sea that made the tide come up about ten times further than the day before," he explains. "We had everything up [the day before], and then right when we started to film, the tide rushed up and washed everything away. And, oddly enough, it was one of those things where it was a blessing and a curse because you go, 'Hold on. The tide just washed everything up and it looks like a shipwreck, so let's leave it.' We left it, so it worked out nicely that as Jamie drags Claire onto the broken piece of wood, that was the final shot of the season."

SEASON FOUR

BUILDING SEASON FOUR: WRITING

America. A new nation promising new beginnings for a myriad of immigrants, including Jamie and Claire Fraser. After two decades of separation and constant movement, they are settling down for the first time in their marriage, on the ten thousand acres of Fraser's Ridge.

"Season four is the theme of home," executive producer Toni Graphia states simply. "From the very first moment in the pilot, when Claire is looking at the vase in the window, all she's ever wanted is a home. Even though she found Jamie, she never really had a home with Jamie, because they were vagabonds." Their exploration of domesticity became the straightfor-

ward spine of the year, which was helpful considering how fraught it was to get the writers' room going while season three was still in active production.

"It was very weird, very challenging, and it almost killed us," Graphia says with a sigh. "There was even talk of hiring a secondary staff to forge ahead and write all the new

episodes while we were still finishing [season three]. But we really wanted the continuity of vision."

Despite the executive producers all being deployed in different areas of production, they just went right into the new season, breaking *Drums of Autumn* into thirteen episodes. "I was in South Africa finishing up [season three] from January till the end of June," executive producer Matt Roberts details. "They started the room in January. What I would do is, I would get notes and I would also do call-ins from South Africa. To say I didn't have a life would be putting it lightly," he laughs. "We tried it really just to shrink the time between seasons to get it out sooner."

In the writers' room, the events in the book worked into episodes rather well overall, Graphia says. "We did more combining and moving things around, but it fell into sections pretty easily," she explains. "We knew it was going to be a slower, quieter season, even though it turned out to have more action than we thought. It's more personal. It's an intimate season. We jokingly called it our *Little House on the Prairie* season because it literally was going to be about homesteads, building the cabin out of nothing."

Moore continues, "The Claire–Jamie story, while they were still in the books and are still interesting characters, the development of them as a couple doesn't really have

the big twists and turns anymore. They were more settled, having a home. At the beginning, I was thinking that [the season] would be much more about pioneering and living up on the Ridge. But there was also a story to service to give the show forward momentum. I think that was a difficult challenge, finding the balance. We had to give Claire and Jamie things to do, which was the new challenge of the series, because there had always been plenty of things for Claire and Jamie to do. This season it was more about what are those things and how do they contribute to a meaningful story at the same time?

"So a lot of the structural stuff was trying to figure out where is Claire in time and space, as a character in this episode?" he continues. "Same thing with Jamie. There were landmarks along the way such as

the Bear Killer, interacting with the tribes, and Jocasta. But trying to knit them together in a way that had a cohesive character arc was definitely a challenge for us through the whole year."

Sometimes it was about finding brand-new moments to build anticipation or surprise around, Matt Roberts explains. "One of the lines that Jamie says in the books is, 'Does the wanting ever stop?' I always like to think that's part of the way the books are constructed and the way we construct the series. Anticipation, to me, is one of the biggest story devices you can use, when people anticipate turning that next page. It's the same thing with telling the story on television. You want the [audience] to wait for that next scene."

The writers were able to turn to Brianna and Roger for a lot of that

anticipation, as the two became major contributors to the narrative. Executive producer Maril Davis admits she was very excited to finally show their stories in detail. "The Roger–Brianna story line is really exciting and interesting because they are going through the early stages of a relationship: getting together, fighting, then being apart and separated. It's ultimately culminating in their handfasting and then being split apart. That has inherent tension and drama to it," she emphasizes.

"And there are certain book moments you're trying to get in every episode," Davis continues about the couple. "Obviously, getting them to the Scottish festival, and certainly the meeting of Jamie and Brianna, it was so important to get that right. I was there the day we filmed those scenes, and I wanted so much to get the essence of that scene right, because so many people have been waiting for it."

Season four was also the year where the series' divergence from the books was the most dramatic to date. "The further you get down the line on an adaptation like this, the more the choices you've made in early years become apparent," Moore explains. "Murtagh not dying at Culloden then creates a different season four. We had talked about bringing Murtagh into the story in year three, and then ultimately we decided it was better in year four. And then we kept moving around

"I was still pretty involved in editorial, almost as much as I was the year before. What was different was that not being in as close contact with production and the day-to-day script changes anymore, I'd be seeing things in editorial that I didn't know or [that] had been changed. There was the whole sequence where Roger and Brianna go to the [festival] in North Carolina. On the first pass in editorial, I remembered what it was on the page, and then I saw it months later in editorial, and I was like, 'Wait a minute, what happened here?' Everything was shot inside the tents, and that was because money was a partial consideration and [as] a result of the weather. I saw it didn't have the scale and the romance. So I made them go out and reshoot it and then add a lot of exterior visuals to it. By the time that I told them to do all that, the weather had improved quite a bit. So it made it much easier, and the burning stag was added in the reshoot."

—RON MOORE

which episode it was going to be. But you keep creating this separation between the books and the on-air show, because the on-air show has to maintain its own integrity about what it's doing. You can't be so tied to the books that then you're contradicting yourself and the mythology that you've created on air."

Heading into the last episodes of the season, the writers doubled down on following their own path, especially in regard to having Murtagh be the element of surprise for book readers. Not only did the writers reveal a relationship between Murtagh and Jocasta, but they also allowed the huge chasm of loyalty—Murtagh to the Regulators and Jamie to the Crown—to be the cliffhanger of the year.

"We always planned to end the season on the other shoe drops and the devil calls in his chip," Graphia says about Jamie getting called on to find and arrest his godfather. "That spins us into next season asking, 'What's Jamie gonna do?'"

"Books and TV are two totally different mediums," Davis says of their changes. "We don't like to end seasons necessarily with everything wrapped in a bow. Even if you know you have two more seasons left, you want people excited to come back the next year. Life is never going to be easy for the Frasers. They're always going to have a tough time," she chuckles.

"You know, this season was daunting at the beginning, but it really came together," Davis assesses in closing. "I'm really proud of it because I think this was a difficult season in terms of story. But there're so many wonderful moments and I'm proud of how it turned out."

BUILDING SEASON FOUR: LOCATIONS AND PRODUCTION DESIGN

How do you shoot one country in substitute for another? That was the conundrum facing the *Outlander* producers, location managers, and production-design team with regards to season four taking place primarily in the American colonies. For a myriad of reasons, it's not an unusual thing for a show to dress a shooting location so thoroughly that they're essentially disguising it as a completely different place. But *Outlander* as a production had not really done that before. With traveling production units, they had ventured to Prague and South Africa, but a lot of the narratives were actually set in Scotland or returned to the country for large chunks of seasons one through three.

Season four was another story, with the Frasers now setting roots in the New World. The *Outlander* production team had spent three seasons building a native infrastructure in Glasgow and the Scottish Highlands, not only at their soundstages but with the talented people who staffed all of their departments. Staying or going somewhere new for production, like the east coast of America, was a huge decision.

Executive producer Matt Roberts flew out to North Carolina in season three to see the terrain for himself in order to inform their decision-making. "I drove around and made sure I walked the terrain and talked to the people there," he says of his reconnaissance. "I went to the eastern band of the Cherokee Nation, their reservation there. I met with the chief, went to the museum there, spoke with people. I drove around the areas that our show plays. The Piedmont, into the Blue Ridge, and just walked the walk. And almost every place I stopped, I was like, 'Scotland can do this. She can play this part.' We always say that Scotland's been a character in *Outlander*, and she really has. She plays North Carolina beautifully, and hats off to Scotland and all the people who make it happen."

It was also the crew that secured the decision in their minds. "At the end of the day, we say it a lot and I think it's a term that some people say is overused, but we really are a family," executive producer Maril Davis explains. "They work so hard for us and we've had a

> *"I brought in Alasdair Walker, who DP'd the first block, and he sets the tone. I said, 'We need to make [this season] look different. It needs to feel like a different place.' It can't feel like Scotland anymore. It has to look and feel like a different place and time, and it has to feel warmer than Scotland feels, so we talked a lot about that."*
>
> —Matt Roberts on changing the light of Scotland to feel more like early America

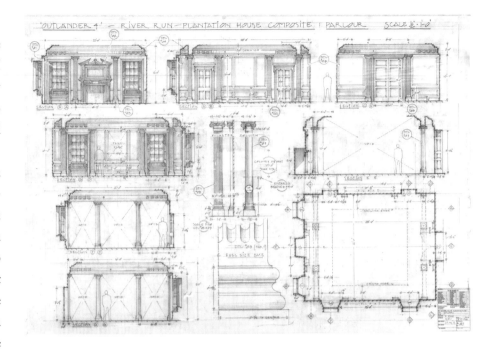

very good retention rate over the years of people coming back. I think the idea of leaving our crew was not something we wanted to consider. We have such a special setup there."

With the decision made, it then fell to producer David Brown, supervising locations manager Hugh Gourlay, production designer Jon Gary Steele, and Matt Roberts to find the places in Scotland that would credibly host sets or double in landscape for what was needed in the season-four narrative. "We were looking at locations in a way that we'd never done before," Brown explains. "You're suddenly excluding Scotland and you're finding North America in Scotland. We had to build a North American street for ourselves, and we were building a part of a plantation house in Scotland. We were looking at every loca-

tion with an eagle eye to make sure there wasn't too much Scotland appearing and suddenly there wasn't some guy in a kilt come around a corner," he jokes.

The standard locations team Gourlay used to fan out and identify specific terrains consisted of twelve people but often bloomed to

twenty as needed. "Season four was more of the model of season one, in that it was about traveling [when] they arrived in America. They're trying to find their wilderness, they're trying to find Fraser's Ridge, so it is much more developing a settlement. In finding those places, one has to be very restricted as to how far you can go, because the production of anything over thirty miles is a cost to production. If you're over an hour away, you then have to accommodate your crew, so the minute you do that, the costs jump considerably.

"And things changed quite a lot the last minute," he continues. "We had weather problems and three days of canceled filming because of snow [when] we were meant to be filming the standing stones so vehicles got stranded up there. We were then having to rejig the schedule, because we couldn't film outside obviously until the snow

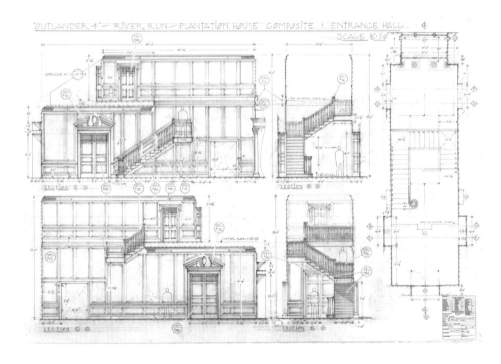

melted. The knock-on effect of that was that we had to bring in other people to change the schedule and juggle that. But like everything else, there's nothing like a good challenge to inspire everyone."

Once the locations were secured, then Steele's team, including set dresser Stuart Bryce, would come in and work their magic on exteriors and interiors to create cohesion across the season's stories. "There is nothing here [in Scotland] that looks like colonial America. Not one little piece," Steele says of what was facing their team. "So we did tons of research and we built a small back lot that has a street for colonial America, which was quite fun. I think that's one of the areas with the most color we've ever used on the sets. I was trying to make it feel like a whole new world, of course, which it does. We went from everything being stone for two to three years to clapboard so that we could play with the color. And we used brighter colors and didn't age the hell out of it like we normally age everything down, because it's a new city."

Outside of the Wilmington set, Steele and his team focused their season-four time on other standing primary sets, including the Mohawk village (detailed in its own chapter), River Run (Jocasta's plantation), and the Frasers' first homestead.

Steele says they did their due diligence on creating an authentic

> *"On season four, I did do a lot of directing on the MRU unit. I didn't do a lot of the title cards this year. I didn't do a lot of the inserts that I normally do. We took on some extra things for Sony, like special scenes for the DVDs; I directed a couple of those. I still directed quite a bit, but it's just I didn't have time to do a whole block of episodes. I'll say I was a little disappointed that I didn't get to, but I know that my time is better used for the show overall."*
>
> —Matt Roberts on how he's shifted responsibilities in making the series

first home built by Jamie, including firsthand research from his own life. "I was raised in Arkansas, and close to where I lived was Prairie Grove Battlefield Park from the Civil War, so there are tons of all kinds of different log cabins," he reveals. "What I remembered the most was the squared-off logs, and I really loved them, so that's the direction I took it. I wanted porches on both the front and the back. And I actually wanted it to be two levels, but I was vetoed on that."

The home was also built on location in an area surrounded by trees, per Steele's vision. "Because this is a new frontier, when they look off their porch or through the window, you should see trees like you're in a forest," Steele says of his visual logic. "It's the New World. They were out in the middle of nowhere, so the location people found a great location that no matter where we looked, we saw trees. We stuck the cabin in the middle. We built a real cabin, inside and out, so it is a real place.

"We had the interior built again onstage because of the light-

ing and the cold," Steele continues of having a more controlled space to shoot. "We have the option of shooting it there on location when they want to open the doors or open the windows and look out. And then we have drops made to match that location around the set onstage. It's all about options."

As for the interior configuration, Bryce says, the cabin has four delineated areas. "There was the bed, which was the bedroom, essentially, there was the apothecary kitchen corner, a dining area, and their little miniature parlor, which was essentially two chairs in front of a fire."

Steele adds that even though it's a one-room cabin, he wanted it to feel functional and creative, considering who lives inside the home. "We squeezed in as much detail as we could. For instance, the first time people went in to look at it, one of the producers said, 'Gary, why does it have two fireplaces?'

"For the Early American standing-stones location, that proved quite an interesting one. We actually found that on an estate down in southwest Scotland. It was just this mound within this beautifully landscaped garden that we obviously had to make less beautiful and less manicured."

—SUPERVISING LOCATIONS
MANAGER HUGH GOURLAY

The reason is this: that one side is Claire's area—her kitchen—where we put all kinds of nooks and crannies, and there're things that she's puttering around [with]. There's a big table in front of it, so that's her domain, which is also what heats the house. On the other side, it's Jamie's, where he sits at night. We have a chair for both of them, where I thought they could sit and have a whisky at night. It's not the kitchen,

it's her own little mini parlor in Jamie and Claire's first home. I'm trying to give them both their space and yet make it feel as warm and cozy as we can."

The other major constructed home of the season is Jocasta's plantation, palatial in comparison to what Jamie and Claire reside in. Since it had to be authentic to the river homes of the era, Steele says, they needed to find a locale that could capture that aesthetic. "People would go up and down the river on these flatbed boats, and the [house] entries would be from the river," Steele says of the historical details. "We were looking for a place that we could build a jetty and have this flatbed wooden boat come up. And we found this one place that had a big pond. There were fields all around it. Some of the producers wanted me to put it in a field because it would've been easier, but I was a bit of a pain," he chuckles. "I wanted it to be between the trees, because I hate it when you see a movie or a TV show and it looks like they dropped the set out in the middle of a field. It looks so fake to me."

The trees would also create a specific framing around the house that Steele wanted to impart to viewers. "You're trying to convey a feel that you're in the South," he explains. "So the greensmen added moss to the tree limbs. We built this big porch that actually was only half a façade." The rest of the porch and the entire second story of River Run were never physically built, instead added in via the magic of visual effects.

As for the interiors, they were all built on the stages, with layers of detail work that Steele says is a direct reflection of Jocasta Cameron's taste and position in society. "I wanted everything to be bronze, or the colors of tobacco, throughout the house, except for those rooms that were slave corridors. But everything changed once we found that blue fabric on those couches."

An expensive fabric find by set decorator Stuart Bryce, it was initially a prohibitive purchase. "But it changes the whole look of the living room, parlor, and the dining room. So we spent the money as it plays for two seasons, and on and on, so it's all worth it," Steele justifies. "Then we used these colors of tobacco for the main foyer, living room, and parlor; it's all shades of tobacco. It's lacquered with Chinese red on the walls, then a layer of gold on top of that. Then many layers of the tobacco colors that get a really thick shellac that makes it look like it's been painted fifty times. And then they rub it with waxes to make it look a little older. We were trying to make it look as rich as it can, because this woman obviously has lots and lots of money. She has good taste, she has money, and she is a powerful woman."

As for the pieces inside the room, Bryce says, "The furniture,

> *"It's very hard to photograph woods. Quite a lot of places were not suitable, as the trees are too straight, or it was too dense, or it wasn't dense enough, or whatever. The other problem of course is the weather and our woodland—it changes a lot during the seasons from winter to summer."*
>
> —HUGH GOURLAY ON THE DIFFICULTY OF FINDING THE RIGHT PLACE FOR FRASER'S RIDGE

the rugs, the drapes, everything was reupholstered, and all the furniture was made. It was made, or some carcass was bought and augmented to make it our own. We took the leap, because the color palette in there's quite unique. Even though it's not a traditional-looking planta-

tion, we worked through the geography of the house and how rooms would have a multipurpose. So pieces could move around within the room, although we had a fairly set and standard layout for stuff, and it all develops from the plan. We did some beautiful paintings, because the information that we had was that she was interested in paintings and art before she lost her sight."

The finished environments all transport the audience to another country, and time, without reproach. "When you look at River Run, it's unbelievable," Davis enthuses. "Between Gary Steele and Stuart, Terry [Dresbach] and Nina [Ayres] and Richard Briscoe and everyone else, I think we have done such a tremendous job of pulling off North Carolina in Scotland."

EPISODE 401: AMERICA THE BEAUTIFUL

WRITERS: MATTHEW B. ROBERTS AND TONI GRAPHIA

DIRECTOR: JULIAN HOLMES

After a grueling season-three production, the *Outlander* writers' room didn't take a customary break for season four. "Matt and I were actually writing and working on 'America the Beautiful' and the [season three] finale at the same time, which is kind of mind-blowing," executive producer/writer Toni Graphia explains.

Done in their typical style of splitting the episode into scenes that they then traded back and forth for notes and redrafts, Roberts says of that script, "We had different ideas to start the season. It was much longer; it was much more lingering, in the sense of not lingering in pace but we spent more time with our characters. It constantly

keeps evolving as you go. When you write on *Outlander*, it's a big bold show, and there's no structure in the sense that there's no formula."

As evidence, Graphia adds that the episode at one point was a two-parter and originally titled "Sea Change." "I had named it that because the [season] takes them to a new world," she says. "But we changed it to 'America the Beautiful' because we realized the season would encompass the whole of America the beautiful, and not so beautiful as well. They'd have to deal with relatives, wild beasts, Americans, and with the corruption."

As the first director of the fourth season, Julian Holmes (*MI-5*) came in early during pre-production to help establish the whole vibe of the new season, which was set in 1767 North Carolina yet being shot in Scotland. "Alasdair Walker, our director of photography, talked fairly extensively about light and about the color of the light that we wanted to reflect in terms of the New World," Holmes explains. "And when we sat down with Matt and Gary [Steele] at the beginning, it was about finding the tone of America. The beginning of America is so important because the difference in our story here is that Jamie and Claire actually have a chance to spend time together. Now it's about family and home-making. So that emotional temperature was taken on board, as well as we've started to look at the colonies as a place of a new future."

But the dark duality of the epi-

> "Bonnet's such a bad guy. We paint him bad, because Ed's such a good-looking boy and such a clean-looking actor. So, there's quite a chance to make him look weathered and grubby and all that. It's always a joy to do that because he's such a good actor. But any way you can help somebody like that be a convincing character, then it's great."
>
> —HAIR AND MAKEUP DESIGNER ANNIE McEWAN ON BONNET'S LOOK

sode title is also reflected in the visuals of the representation of the Native American stone ceremony, and then the hangman's noose in the scene right after. "It was really important to us that when we started the story, we were starting the story from inside," Holmes explains. "It was best to see it from, more or less, Jamie's point of view at the beginning, so we start with the hanging and that takes us straight to the heart of the set piece in the middle of the town square of Wilmington."

> *"Some of the approaches to extending Wilmington [with VFX] were borrowing the same techniques we had done with the Royal Mile, which in turn had borrowed from Versailles in season two."*
>
> —VFX SUPERVISOR RICHARD BRISCOE

In the first ten minutes of the episode, Jamie and audiences also meet the series' new antagonist, Stephen Bonnet (Ed Speleers). Graphia found him to be an incredibly interesting villain. "He's a thief, an outlaw, and a pirate, but he's more interesting because he has more psychological layers. We get to know his backstory, about how he became this man who relies on luck."

In translating the character to the series, Graphia and Roberts made some adjustments to Bonnet's focus. "In the book, he's fascinated with Jamie, but we thought that's been done, and we shifted his focus to Claire," she details. "Matt and I added the scene where Claire's stitching his wound and he's talking about drowning and his fears, because we want them to commiserate. You know that Claire had just almost died [in the ocean]. He's kind of like a sociopath prying into her psyche to forge a connection with her."

Bonnet then uses what he's learned observationally, and situa-

> "The moment when we do finally talk about [Ian's assault] is in a graveyard, while they're digging a grave for someone. It's so dramatic. For Jamie, it's been a long time for him now, and time heals. But he still has those scars, physically and mentally. He understands the place that Young Ian's at. I think he's always been a real love of Jamie's. He's quite like his son, in a way."
>
> —SAM HEUGHAN ON THE SCENE WITH IAN

tionally, about the Frasers to violently rob them on their river journey to Jocasta Cameron's home. A unique sequence in the history of the series, it was scored by Ray Charles's classic rendition of "America the Beautiful."

"Instead of just doing a generic robbery scene, we came up with the idea to do it under a song," Graphia imparts. "We originally thought we would score it, but somewhere in the postproduction it was decided to use the Ray Charles version because it's so soulful. We didn't think at the time it was controversial. We just thought it was a cool, creative choice. And absolutely we were not being political. We never write with politics in mind."

In fact, during production the music wasn't played, not even to set the tone in the moment. Holmes says they were instead concerned with finding the terror in the act, despite a very small shooting space. "There were issues because [that riverboat is] such a small set for us to work in. We did a lot of that green screen, so we didn't actually put a boat on the river. A lot of it was done in a studio. We made sure that we didn't have huge cameras in there. We'd have to obviously use slightly wider lenses just to help that feeling of claustrophobia." But when the song was eventually cut to the footage, Holmes says, "the music fights against it deliberately in such a way to say that this America is not the

> "In the book, Frank's ring is taken [by Bonnet]. We thought it would be more heartbreaking for Jamie's ring to be taken. And it would also give us an opportunity to get the new ring, so then we get two rings. We get the amazing Lallybroch ring, which we all love because it was cool, and he gets to make another ring for her. We designed a new ring. We didn't have it match exactly the ring that was described in the book, because it's handmade. It had to look like it was authentically made by a silversmith in that era. So the ring is similar in description, but it's a more rough-hewn version."
>
> —TONI GRAPHIA

America that we think it's going to be. This world, this New World, with all its new promise, is not going to be as easy as they think it might be."

EPISODE 402: DO NO HARM

WRITER: KAREN CAMPBELL DIRECTOR: JULIAN HOLMES

Outlander has never shied away from depicting terrifically upsetting moments that happen to, or around, Claire and Jamie Fraser. For the Frasers' arrival at Jocasta Cameron's River Run plantation in "Do No Harm," the writers decided to explore the institution of slavery with a personal framing. "We talked a great deal about authentically portraying the horrors of slavery

> "We did have rehearsal time, even with the smaller moments—when you first meet Phaedre, and the looks between her and Claire when she sees her for the first time. So I felt as if there was a weight put on the importance of these meetings and these new characters."
>
> —NATALIE SIMPSON

and knew that this episode was going to have gut-wrenchingly violent sequences," co-executive producer/writer Karen Campbell explains.

"I'm of mixed-race heritage, so I felt very drawn to that particular story line," director Julian Holmes adds. "Without being overly intellectual about it, the idea of going upriver and landing somewhere that feels like a peaceful paradise, that

turns into something quite horrific, was really a powerful story."

Campbell says the script went through a lot of redrafting to achieve the right impact. "There was an initial draft written that had Rufus dying in the middle—once Jamie and Claire reach the lumber camp—staying true to how it unfolded in the source material."

The executive producers and writing staff eventually decided to place his death at the end of the episode. "We re-broke the episode as a result and I rewrote it," Campbell details. "Ultimately, in my opinion, the rewrite wound up enriching the story because it gave us more time

> "Sam I've known for many years. In fact, I cast him in one of his first TV shows. It was for a show I did called Party Animals for BBC Two. It was great because I saw Sam then, and I know the Sam here and now, and I promise you that he's the same man and it's brilliant."
>
> —Director Julian Holmes on his history with Sam Heughan

with Rufus, making his death all the more heartbreaking and tragic in the end. It also gave us a tremendous scene between Ulysses and

Claire that didn't exist in the prior iteration where Ulysses attempts to lay out the peril Claire's actions are putting the other slaves in."

Holmes was also pleased they were able to get across how much the acceptance of the institution had already sunk into the culture of North Carolina. "We'd be very careful about Jocasta and her politics around what she sees to be as staff, even though they're essentially a commodity. It was about the reality of her world being 'It is what it is.' Jocasta is a product of that particular time. It was a tricky, tricky tightrope to walk for us," he says with gravity. "But I think for me, the

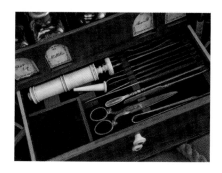

"Slavery is a thing here [in America], and his reaction to that is one of just bafflement. Especially when it comes to River Run, which is, ironically, incredibly beautiful. But then behind it, there is so much blood. When he finally sees that firsthand, I think that's another really key moment in Ian's figuring out who he is and what he stands for in his own world."

—JOHN BELL

whole idea of the laws, and how they enact the laws, and how the landowners seek retribution, it felt very truthful to me."

Because of Rufus's punishment and then the lynching scene in the last act, it was a script that took a lot out of Campbell. "This was the darkest episode I've ever written. It stirred up all kinds of emotions—anger, horror, sorrow, more anger, more sorrow, more horror. It was an

"The site [for River Run] was already a given when I started. But nothing was there. We looked at this field by the water—and, incidentally, it's not a river. It's a pond, essentially, but it sort of looked like a river. I stood there with Gary [Steele] and we put some traffic cones down and said, 'All right, here's where we're going to put the house.' The strangest thing about that decision is that there was a tree growing out in the middle of it. A great big massive oak tree right in the middle of where we wanted the house to be. So all the interior stuff is a set back at Cumbernauld at the studios. We blue-screened the entire top [floor], all the bedrooms, and the roof."

—DIRECTOR JULIAN HOLMES

incredibly visceral experience writing the script and imagining what life was like for those involved and enslaved in the plantation system during this ugly time in our history. Then to be on set witnessing the script being performed by our actors and supporting artists, who all did outstanding work, brought

on more gut-wrenching feelings—and we were only giving the tiniest glimpse into what life was like for so many slaves, who lived that nightmare every day."

She continues, "The scenes that made me the most emotional while writing the script were the ones with Rufus; imagining what

life must have been like for him would bring tears to my eyes. I thought about my brother and sister and how heartbreaking it would be to be forcibly separated from them at such a young age and thrust into a living nightmare, yet still remembering the good times with them, then wondering where they were taken, how they were doing, and if I'd ever see them again, in this life or what comes after. Jerome Holder was outstanding in the role. His portrayal of Rufus was imbued with such warmth and sadness. And Julian Holmes did an excellent job. We were incredibly fortunate to have him aboard."

Despite the bleak and uncompromising visual, Holmes says, "I'm particularly proud of the end. It feels like a very emotionally brutal, devastating, and powerful ending, with the way that the traders treat the slaves and the idea of what the law meant at that time as well, and the way people behaved."

SPOTLIGHT

SOPHIE SKELTON AS BRIANNA RANDALL FRASER

I n the season-two finale, "Dragonfly in Amber," audiences got a crash introduction to twenty-year-old Brianna Randall. Raised as the daughter of Claire and Frank Randall, Bree has her world turned upside down with that episode by the revelations of her true parentage, discovering the existence of time travel, and meeting the future love of her life, Roger Wakefield.

Actress Sophie Skelton relished the challenge but was more than ready to get a few more episodic hours in *Outlander's* third season to flesh Brianna out. The narrative rewinds to show Bree in her late teens leading up to age twenty, so there's more context and perspective for what she's been through in her young life. "In season three, Bree matures a little bit," Skelton says, assessing her character. "But she's still reeling from the death of Frank, and she's obviously taken that in a very bad way. She feels responsible, but for Bree it does come across in a very Fraser-like way. She is quite stoic, quite hotheaded, and

can come across as quite stern, which on Jamie Fraser might look very sexy but on a young, teenage girl can look a bit bratty." She smiles knowingly. "It's quite interesting the way that the similar traits show differently."

The small block of episodes featuring Bree did allow for more of a mother–daughter rapport, which was limited to being strained in season two. "What was done lovely about season three is that you see that Claire and Brianna have sort of closed the gap that they've had between them for the past twenty years," the actress explains. "So when Bree sends Claire back, there was almost this mother–daughter role reversal, and I thought it showed a side of Bree that we hadn't really seen until that point."

There's also more quality time given to Roger and Bree, to establish how different they truly are yet still bound by this extraordinary knowledge about Claire and a deep attraction to each other. Skelton says for a young woman whose life is in turmoil, there's a lot to be

confused about. "It's almost like holiday romances, where you get caught up in the moment and the distraction of everything now," she says of Bree's hesitant feelings toward Roger. "You can wrongly associate certain feelings with a person as opposed to a situation, so she's just trying to be careful. In a way, she's perfectly justified. You look at people who come from broken homes, and stereotypically they have a certain outlook on marriage that maybe people who came from happy homes don't."

A deeper exploration of those issues gets put on hold until season four, when Brianna and Roger are brought back into the narrative for good in "The False Bride." The audience gets reacquainted with them as they too spend time together after a year apart. It's romantic and sweet, and then it goes horribly wrong when their communication problems rear up once more.

"I know that the scene in the cabin obviously had a lot of split opinions, and there is no right or wrong, but I do also think that Bree, in this moment, is being more mature really than we've seen her before," Skelton asserts about Bree's decision not to accept Roger's proposal. "Actually, I think she's being very calculated. She does love Roger, so it's a selfless move that she's not getting swept into it too quickly. She wants to make sure that she doesn't hurt him further down the line. Or vice versa. I think what we forget is that Bree has lost a lot of people in a few years, and she's really in self-preservation mode. She wants to make sure Roger's not going to leave her either.

"And [sleeping with Roger] is a big move for her,

not only because she is a virgin but because Roger isn't," Skelton continues. "He has slept with other women, and I think for Bree it would be a lot more straightforward if he hadn't. If it's just a question of his morals, that's fine. But I feel you can't pick and choose your morals, and I think, in that moment, she really did think that he was being terribly hypocritical."

Their fight and separation ends up freeing Brianna to make some decisions on her own when she discovers that her mother and Jamie will be in mortal danger in their time, so she makes the call to travel through the stones to warn them herself. "I do feel that season four is where Bree comes into her own a lot, and you actually see her personality properly," Skelton says, citing that moment as an example.

Her mettle is tested when she crosses through in "Down the Rabbit Hole," but the actress says she cherished showing Bree go through it all with determination. "She's made this decision, she's strong; she's afraid but she's going to power through and see it through no matter what cost. And I think even though she goes back with all the knowledge of the past, she's going back more educated than Claire did, because she made the decision to go. She knows enough about history and about the past to know the decorum of the time and the risks. But she doesn't quite think it's going to go how it does."

In particular, one of the defining moments in Bree's

entire narrative is her rape at the hands of Stephen Bonnet. Despite the series confronting that vile act in many scenarios, Skelton says she felt the deep responsibility of playing the moment with authenticity and with repercussions. "I've actually met a few ladies at conventions who said that they were petrified to see it because they have been victims of rape," she says soberly. "I really wanted to do [it] in a way to bring justice to women who have been through it. You want them to almost feel some kind of catharsis at the end of it, by going through the trauma with Bree and seeing Bree come out the end of it and feel like, 'Wow, there's a light at the end of the tunnel for me too.'"

While "Wilmington" showed only the beginning of Bonnet's assault, Skelton was adamant about making sure subtle details remained that would help create context. "Initially, when Bree goes into that room [with Bonnet], they wanted me closing the door. But I was like, 'Bree going into that room to ask for the ring is not that unreasonable, but her shutting the door behind herself isn't something that I think a savvy sixties girl would do.' We made sure that it's [Bonnet] who slams the door later, because Bree wouldn't lock herself in a room. She's more worldly and streetwise than that. I wanted to make you feel that Bree kept her distance with him and it was a very stern 'Let's get this business done so I can leave.' And Ed plays a very good Bonnet,

in terms of luring people into this false sense of charm—a honey trap almost."

Then, just one episode later in "The Birds and The Bees," Skelton needs to shift emotional gears one hundred eighty degrees to play the other defining moment of Bree's young life: meeting Jamie Fraser.

"You want to do justice to the fans in terms of what they want to see," Skelton says of the anticipated scene, "but at the same time we can't have this grand reunion of Bree and Jamie falling into each other's arms, because realistically we are not in that mindset. I think where she does fall into his arms, that's really more relief, like, 'Oh my goodness, you're a part of my mother, and I need

131

her right now.' And also there's relief that he's accepted her in a way that Laoghaire put into Bree's mind that he wouldn't. Bree [is] collapsing on him as I think she would collapse on anyone she knew at that point. She needs a familiar face and a hug. There are so many things going through her head at that point. She's so fresh from the rape, I mean, it was only the night before!"

Brianna's emotions aside, that moment with Jamie also signified Skelton's first scene playing against Sam. "It was quite funny, because obviously we've done press together for two years and everything else, but we hadn't properly worked together," she says, laughing at the absurdity. Luckily, from that moment on, the pair got a lot of scenes, which she loved playing with Heughan. But placing Bree with her parents also put her back in scenes with Caitriona Balfe, which she says was like coming home.

"When they have that reunion, it's just lovely," Skelton says with genuine emotion. "You really see how much they mean to each other, and from then on, Claire almost becomes Bree's best friend. She's the only one who knows everything that's going on with Bree. She talks about the pregnancy, about the rape, and Claire really does become her confidante. They become a little team. Claire knows what's going on with Bree before Bree has to say it, which shows how far the mother–daughter relationship has come."

That connection has a tremendous impact on whom Brianna decides she wants to be going forward, as evidenced when she chooses to confront Stephen Bonnet in "Providence." Skelton says even she had to wrap her head around the divisive choice to play it. "[Bree's choice] was one of those things where I feel she must just be a better person than me, because if it was me, I think I would probably go to the prison and kill him," she says candidly. "I really wanted to get into Bree's mindset . . . but I couldn't get my head into her head, because I honestly can't understand giving him that gift. So I delved into the web and found YouTube videos of women actually in court cases, reading letters to their attacker. It was really heartbreaking, because their attacker is ten meters away from them and they're reading these forgiveness letters. There's *so* much strength in that," she emphasizes. "For women to go through it is one thing, but to be able to forgive someone is just really admirable. I ended up just crying in my apartment on my own for like two hours as I was watching these interviews that just really affected me."

Skelton says she carried all of that into the scene with her. "On the walk up to the cell, I wanted Bree to be quite petrified, almost shaking, because it's like she's reliving the trauma. Then, before she goes into the cell, she steels herself because she's so determined to not let him see how much she's been affected.

"There was this one take we did," she remembers quietly. "I don't know what came over me, but I was just getting so angry at Bonnet, I just started crying. You know when you're shaking, trying to catch your breath, because you're so angry? It's almost like those women were speaking through me. I just saw red. They used a more stripped-back-anger version, because I do think that they wanted it more as a straightforward forgiveness. But there's a lot of colors in that scene. I even love when she's made her peace, she's ready to leave, and he just makes one more little remark and then Bree turns and the whole thing starts again. It's just great; it was a really well-written scene."

It's an empowering moment for Bree, but it can't release her from the shackles of the times and living in River Run. Despite the generosity of Jocasta toward

her, Skelton says, "I wanted to play that Bree's feeling very boxed in, and she must be feeling so empty. All she can do in those days is what women did—sit and draw and drink tea. All Bree wants to do is get on a horse and go and find Roger," she says determinedly. "And with the slavery element, just the same way that Claire can't stomach it, Bree's the same. But then there's that hard inner battle in terms of there's nothing we can do. I *never* wanted it to look like she's just settling into Aunt Jocasta's life and agreeing with it and that's why she's staying. I wanted to make sure that people know that she's almost being held prisoner, in a way. She has made friends with the slaves because she's not okay with that world and in a very difficult position. I think the saving grace is having Lord John Grey there."

By "Man of Worth," Brianna is a mother, she's survived her darkest days, and she knows whom she wants to be with as Roger comes back to her at River Run. They've both run their own personal gauntlets and are now irrevocably changed. Skelton says that's why she and Rankin wanted to play their coming together with weight, not just passion. "She can't read him at all, he's not giving her anything, and it's only when he says 'I love you' that Bree's like, 'Oh my goodness, thank you. You're here. For me.' It's a very Brianna–Roger reunion, falling into each other's arms, yet it's still a 'What does this mean? Where are we?' sort of moment. It plays really nicely, that sweeping shot is good . . . and running in those skirts is very difficult," she laughs, knowing that's the least of the worries yet to come.

EPISODE 403: THE FALSE BRIDE

WRITER: JENNIFER YALE DIRECTOR: BEN BOLT

In the third episode of the season, "The False Bride," the writers found the right place to weave Brianna and Roger back into the narrative. Co–executive producer Luke Schelhaas says the convergence of Jamie and Claire in 1767 traveling to Fraser's Ridge for the first time while Brianna and Roger travel to Grandfather Mountain for the Scottish festival in 1970 worked well for their purposes.

"Just to finally get to the Roger–Brianna relationship, it's such good stuff," Schelhaas enthuses. "The romance that develops between them over the course of this day at the festival, and then the really unfortunate way that it ends, it's great structure for an episode. And it's a great launching pad for them for this season."

Despite a script that jumped back and forth in time, director Ben Bolt (*Vikings*) says the visual transition points were clear for him. "Whenever I direct anything, I'm always trying to imagine the effect it's going to have on a first-time viewer, so one starts to imagine in one's head what those two things would look like juxtaposed together. You make lots of tiny little choices and decisions, not just in the look of it but in the way that it's performed."

"We exaggerated the seventies [aesthetic] a little bit from the reference that we found to make it feel more like the show. The spaces that we put Roger and Brianna in, we pretty much stuck close to the color palettes of the time. We had catalogs from the period that have tons of popular culture and modern, of-the-time bits and pieces in there. It was leaving the mid-century period and getting a bit more into the sixties and seventies."

—SET DECORATOR STUART
BRYCE ON DRESSING THE
SEVENTIES-ERA SETS

The scene that was universally exciting for the creatives and actors to bring to life was Brianna and Roger's romantic evening that turns sour. "They're having a very sympathetic time with each other and it develops into this flaming row, where they end up thinking they're not going to see each other in the near future, if ever again," Bolt details. "We rehearsed that, which is a terrific luxury in episodic television. We talked about the characters' intentions and what the shape through the scene was, and then we started to rehearse it and block it, so that by the time we arrived on the location we were pretty thoroughly prepared for that one."

"It's a really compelling scene," Schelhaas adds. "You get to know a lot about the characters. I thought those two were fantastic in that scene where they really fight. It makes you heartbroken, and you're

screaming at the screen. 'C'mon, you can make up!'" he faux-yells in frustration. "But I think it's real. People do that. They walk away in the middle of a fight, and if they hadn't, the future would've been very different."

Bolt agrees about Skelton and Rankin's work. "They are particu-

larly good. I think Sophie's so fresh in that scene, her surprise and genuine confusion. It's not like she's acting. You really feel this girl doesn't know what's going on and she's having to make it up as she

"There's the scene where Roger's sitting in the empty manse playing [guitar], and that meant a lot to me. He's playing one of the tracks he plays at the festival, and that was quite important for me because that was a reflection of who he is and his life there. The track he plays is quite nippy on the fingers and, to me, was loaded with sentiment. [I thought] he and the Reverend played that song, or he taught him that song. [The producers] wanted me to be serenading it to Brianna and looking at her. But Roger is playing that music for himself, and at the festival there's a Scottish history that is a whole other side of his life. I think there's a moment of connection, but I was playing it for Roger within himself."

—RICHARD RANKIN ON
THE BACKSTORY OF ROGER'S
GUITAR PLAYING

goes along. I think she's brilliant in the scene."

Meanwhile, in the past, Jamie and Claire experience a storm-filled night of separation that lays the groundwork for one of the series' most supernatural moments: when a ghostly Native American reveals himself to Claire. "Matt took the lead on this creatively, and as far as I recall, he never wanted it to feel tricksy," Bolt says about the execution of Claire "seeing" the Indian vision in the storm. "He wanted it to be otherworldly, but he didn't want there to be transparent ghostly figures or any kind of morphing. We engineered a route for the guy where he wouldn't get wet, so there he is, with his torch and his dry clothes in the middle of a rainstorm. It was a decision in post to make him disappear. We didn't think about it during the shoot, that during lightning flashes he could disappear momentarily and reappear, but we undersold that rather than oversold it."

The writers then connected it to the huge moment that closes the

"The very first image of the season is the American standing stone cairns being built by an ancient American people, to set up what's coming. We're doing American stones now. But you don't know watching it how those stones are gonna come back into play. Then the first indication of how it comes back into play is by Claire finding this skull and seeing the ghost who she assumes is the ghost of a Mohawk man and later seeing those fillings. It's such a chilling moment when you realize there is another time traveler and it's not just [her]. It's not just Geillis. And it's not just over in Scotland. When she shows Jamie the fillings, he says, 'Well, there must be a place like Craigh na Dun nearby.' Now the audience is saying, 'Okay, when are we gonna see those?'"

—LUKE SCHELHAAS

episode, where Jamie and Claire decide to take Tryon's land offer and pick the location for their new home in what will be Fraser's Ridge. "We—for a number of interesting reasons and conversations in the room—brought it forward [in the story] and made it part of their journey to Fraser's Ridge," Schelhaas explains. "We took it from the book, but we put it in a different context, that she follows those footsteps and that's what brings her back to Jamie. So somehow this ghost, this time traveler, led them to Fraser's Ridge. It's a nice moment to come to at the end of that episode."

"Caitriona is always so on the money that you don't think, Here's an actress standing under a rain machine watching another actor pretend to be a ghost. *You think,* This is a woman in the woods in pioneering America, and she's got this relationship with this ghost. *She is extraordinary because she wasn't frightened of it, yet she was respectful and awed by it. It must take a lot of strength of character to do that time after time after time. She was out there, and it was freezing cold."*

—DIRECTOR BEN BOLT ON
CAITRIONA SELLING CLAIRE'S
VISION OF OTTER-TOOTH

SPOTLIGHT

RICHARD RANKIN AS
ROGER WAKEFIELD MACKENZIE

When audiences meet Roger Wakefield MacKenzie in the season-two episode "Dragonfly in Amber," hearts break a bit for the sweet young man who just lost his father. He is bookish, gentle, and sad, and it's no wonder Claire and her daughter, Brianna, are taken by his kind manner and earnest charm. Their fateful meeting at Reverend Wakefield's wake sweeps the historian into an unbelievable search through time that fully entwines Roger in the main narrative by seasons three and four.

Knowing the epic ride Roger will experience, per the books, gave actor Richard Rankin a lot of patience for the initial slow rollout of his character's journey. "Season three was quite nice because it was sandwiched between pitching him in season two and where he goes in season four, so that was going to be my last opportunity to play Roger properly at home," the actor says of revealing Roger's roots. "One of the things that really

got me about Roger, especially in season three, was that he's still very much distracted by Claire and Brianna. He's also surrounded by mythology and mysticism and magic, which is Roger's jam," he chuckles. "But what is underneath all of that is he's quite lonely. He doesn't really have an anchor; he doesn't really have a home. His father had died not long ago, and Brianna and Claire had very much temporarily filled a void."

Rankin quickly identified what a heady distraction that would be for someone raised as conservatively as Roger was, and he played into it. "He's been utterly engulfed in something fascinating," he says of Claire's incredible story. "The work that he's been doing there has been something he's never done before as a historian. So how do you flesh that out? How do you go about your day under those circumstances?"

While Roger and Brianna's stories don't play into the season-three narrative after "Freedom & Whisky,"

Rankin says he spent a lot of time between seasons thinking about how the weight of what Roger experiences with Claire's time travel and his burgeoning feelings for Bree change him leading into season four. "You build a huge relationship with your character, so I like to refresh at the start of every season," he says of his process. "I take myself away. I figure out where I was at. You can carry the weight of that [backstory] into a scene. When you see Roger again in season four, I think there's definitely more of a weight to him immediately. Something has slightly changed. Whether or not you can put your finger on it, it doesn't matter, but that's important for me to bring that in."

Rankin says he and Sophie Skelton also talked a lot together about fleshing out the off-camera dynamics of Roger and Bree leading into "The False Bride." "We spoke at considerable length about when they communicated, what they talked about, how often did they see each other, because we realize there's a gap," he explains. "I'm not happy with our year-and-a-half gap without knowing what happened with them, then just jumping straight back in, to 'I love you and I want to marry you,'" he says with incredulity. "[Knowing all of

that] helps me arrive at how to play what we did later on in season four. I think it's important to bring those things into the mix—all of the baggage and the journeys of each of the characters that has brought them to that point."

More important, they also figured out what keeps Roger and Brianna so connected when all of the madness rains down on them in season four. "Sophie and I talk all of the time of the thing that keeps them strong together, and it's just that unbreakable, truly unique bond that they've forged with each other at the end of season two. There's a real strength in that," he emphasizes. "But I think oftentimes Brianna and Roger are aware of that, and what they're asking is, 'What do we do with this thing?' It's something unfinished, it's something, somewhere deep in your soul, you know that is going to come to fruition."

Believing in that unseen tether between them made it easier for Rankin to play the more combustible moments between the two, which on the surface are so contrary to either character's true intentions, like their big fight at the Highlands festival. "You know, I can justify that Roger did what he did, and his general outlook on life and marriage and love, because I went through that process with him," he says of the frustration even he had for the duo. "I know who the man is and how he views the world. I also know how Brianna views the

world—so does Roger, but he kind of overlooks that briefly," he chuckles.

But, in general, Rankin believes and plays Roger as loving Brianna and always wanting her to be okay, which is why he chases her across time. "Logic sometimes goes out the window when you're led by the heart," Rankin says with a smile. "But he's terrified for Brianna. This girl, as strong as she is, as modern as she is, she's throwing herself into the eighteenth century, and that's not good. How does she get from Inverness even over to the Carolinas? A lady like Brianna, she's striking, she's beautiful. Your eyes are immediately drawn to her, so she's going to attract attention, and that's what Roger is thinking. So he's going to take that step and he's going to go back. I can't imagine if he stops to think about it for very long [or] if he thinks the outcome for either of them is going to be very good, because he's not equipped to deal with that either," he sighs. "He's a fish out of water, but that's what brings so much of the drama to it. Listen, if Roger was anyone else, he'd be dead. He'd be off the back of the *Gloriana*, if he ever made it on it."

Beyond all odds, each of them makes it to Wilmington and, by fate, runs into the other, in a reunion that is both romantic and fiery. "I think that's a fated moment for them," Rankin offers. "It was very important for us to be aware of the importance of the delicacy

of that and what that means and what that means to them. That scene and the following consummation, Sophie and I had talked about at great lengths. We knew it was coming. We had known it had been coming for a couple of years. I think they need that. It gives them a sense of place. It's a huge milestone for Roger and Brianna. It's also a very beautiful moment. It's also finally that commitment to each other that I think was maybe inevitable."

Of the handfasting, Rankin says, "It finally gets Roger the foundation he requires, and he would love no other more than Brianna. And I think the intimacy of that—you don't want to overplay it but just try to give it a sense of the culmination of all of these things in that moment. That coming together of the two of them was very important for me. And it's a huge tease as well, because we want to have built their relationship up to the point where the audience screams at the TV, 'Just do it,'" he laughs. "'Just get together, please; my nerves can't take it.'"

As we know, their moment of bliss doesn't even last the night, when truths come out that create a monumental row that has Bree kicking Roger out. "The anger comes when you have a moment when you connect with somebody, then that fear just starts coming in," he says of the psychology of that fight. "You find a reason

to push somebody away, because she watched her parents have such a poor relationship. That can be quite a subconscious, unwilling thing that happens."

For the rest of season four, Rankin worked with new scene partners, including bookended fight scenes with Sam Heughan. "Yeah, two fights," he says, smiling. "That sets up quite an intense, unpredictable relationship for them both." But regardless, the actor was just grateful to finally play some scenes with Heughan. "It was like Sam Heughan works on this other thing that's set in the Highlands of Scotland with warriors and shit and I'm on this sixties TV show," Rankin jokes. "So it's always been something I've been hugely excited about, working with Sam and starting to work with a wider part of the cast."

Rankin also loved playing against Yan Tual for the Father Alexandre scenes in "Providence," which really pushed Roger's worldview even more. "There's a lot of similarities between those two characters, and that's how and why they connect," Rankin explains. "Roger has so much compassion for him because he can see the reasons for the things that he's doing, but he's certainly

ahead of that game. That's why Roger says, 'No, just stop what you're doing; I know exactly what path you're going down here. Trust me, I know because I have done it and it doesn't work out well. Look after yourself or else it's not going to end well for you. I know because I'm about one step ahead of where you are right now, and it's not worth it.' Also, Alexandre's trying to be the martyr, and Roger can't get his head around it."

Getting to play out that story to its tragic conclusion—as Roger escapes but returns after hearing Alexandre's screams—and then witness the couple's sacrifice is a moment he most admires about his character. "Through that whole journey, he's like, 'I'm all about me. I'm going to start looking after number one.' But one of the first things he does is, as he escapes for like the ninth time, he goes back! It's like, 'You talk a good game, Roger, and I think you want to be that selfish person that looks after himself, but you don't have it in you.'"

The actor says it was important in that moment to see what about Roger is still the same good man but also see all of the core changes that are part of him too. "All you have to do is replay all these moments for yourself and what that means to you, and what that means to the character will come out in the playing of that. At the end of the day, just going through that journey for Roger and allowing it to come out was enough, because it was so well written. But it was also necessary for Roger to go through this little journey of realization for himself and I suppose to emphasize how he's changed through the fourth season and to set him up in a way that's going to give us a good platform going forward with Roger.

"That was one of my biggest objectives," he says, reflecting on the two-season journey. "To make sure that Roger comes out at the end of season four a vastly different guy from what we met. It was really important for him to acknowledge that. He can't move on, really, without going through that process, without taking that journey, or without being aware of that journey. I feel like he can move on as a character and can build upon that."

EPISODE 404: COMMON GROUND

WRITER: JOY BLAKE DIRECTOR: BEN BOLT

Once Jamie signs his agreement with Governor Tryon for ten thousand acres of land at the top of "Common Ground," the episode proceeds to split the narrative between an estranged Brianna and Roger in 1971 and the construction of the Fraser homestead in 1770.

According to co-executive pro-

ducer Luke Schelhaas, the writers' room wanted the Frasers to have to confront another issue present in their new home: the Native Americans who were there long before them. "The Cherokee in the episode feel like they're too close, and they kind of want to let them know that. The title, 'Common Ground,' gives you that sense that we're going to

have to learn to live next to each other and be good neighbors. That's what Jamie and Claire want. And ultimately we find out that's what the Cherokee want as well. But you would have to prove yourself in some way, and that's the genesis of this story."

Another sensitive topic to traverse in the narrative, Schelhaas says, "Our intention was always that Tryon was clearly giving them land that was the king's land based on a prior treaty. I think there are viewers who reacted to the sense that Jamie and Claire were taking

ten thousand acres of Cherokee land and were asking why would Claire be okay with that. That may not have been completely clear on the screen, but our intention was they were not taking Indian land.

> "We didn't have the time or the budget to do something like *The Revenant*. So then we had to look at if there was North American black bear in the U.K., [to train] to be around Sam Heughan and not maim him. The decision was so easy to make: We're not doing that. We just don't have enough time to make it safe for the actual actor and the crew. We then borrowed from one book and re-created a story to try to keep it in the spirit of seeing Jamie fight a real bear. That's a perfect example of something that you can do in a book but something you can't practically do in a television series."
>
> —MATT ROBERTS ON WHY THEY CHANGED THE BEAR
> FIGHT FOR THE TV SERIES

There was a treaty between the Crown and the Cherokee people—and that's referenced in a later episode—so this was the Crown's land. And there's a treaty line; don't go beyond it. From there, everybody can rightfully have their own opinion about whether that treaty was just, historically."

Meanwhile, Brianna and Roger's scenes are primarily about what the two aren't saying to each other after their fight in North Carolina. Roger discovers proof in historical records that Jamie and Claire reunited and had a life together, so he calls to tell Bree but doesn't give her the whole story.

Director Ben Bolt was a fan of how the duo played their long-distance conversations: "I thought that Sophie took the news on the phone very well from Richard." Getting to direct the pair over two episodes, he says, "Once we got to know each other a little bit, which didn't take very long, they were very inclusive [with me]. They were the final arbiters of what their characters were like, frankly, and I think that's appropriate, because they're going to play them long after I'm gone. But they were very receptive

Bear
Man
54

TDresbach
2017

"I'm the most relieved, is
probably the best word, that we
pulled off the bear-killer
sequence. That was torturing all
of us. I just knew in my gut,
from the very beginning, there's
no way we're going to be able to
do this bear fight with Jamie,
which is such a key moment in
the book. I think it was Toni
Graphia who came up with the
idea of the American Indian
having gone mad out in the
woods and dressing like a bear.
At first, there was a lot of debate
internally, but we just committed
to it. Terry [Dresbach] did an
amazing costume that sold it,
with the big claws. It had to be
shot in a certain way so it didn't
give it away. The stunt work had
to be just so, and at the end of
the day, though, it worked."

—RON MOORE

to my input and suggestions and direction."

"The thing that we embrace on this show is that there is an element of serendipity," Schelhaas details about their unfolding story. "Roger finds this obituary and, for whatever reason, decides not to tell Brianna. What we don't know, and what we play offscreen later, is that Brianna has found it as well. The only reason why we know that is that Frank had found it. She saw it but didn't know what it was. I remember having discussions [in the writers' room] of, do we want to know that she found it? Or do we want that to be a surprise? We eventually decided to play it through Roger's perspective, and that was done from the audience's

perspective, so there was a great shock at the end of the episode, hopefully."

Back on Fraser's Ridge, the big action sequence of the episode happens when the banished Cherokee warrior Tskili Yona (Flint Eagle), who is stalking the woods in a huge bearskin, is killed by Jamie. Of the heavily reworked story from the book, Bolt admits, "I remember being anxious about whether we could sell this 'Bear Man' without it being an anticlimax when we revealed who he was. But I think it was a smart thing to do, because everyone was going to judge it against *The Revenant*."

The director says in preparation for the sequence, "I talked to the stunt coordinator a couple of

weeks before we were shooting and described the beats that I would like in the fight. He took Sam and the Cherokee stunt guy off, rehearsed with them. They videotaped it and showed it back to me. We discussed that and made a few tweaks to it, so, again, when they arrived on the night, they knew what they were doing. [Cinematographer] Stijn Van der Veken's lighting helped that [scene] in the woods, so I thought that sight was frightening enough, and it worked."

SPOTLIGHT

Maria Doyle Kennedy as

Jocasta Cameron

By season four of *Outlander*, it had been some time since we last met any new members of Jamie's immediate family. In fact, only one of his maternal relatives is still alive, the famed Jocasta Cameron, who left Scotland to start anew in North Carolina. When Jamie and Claire also find themselves in the colonies, a family reunion opens the season at Jocasta's plantation, River Run.

As it turns out, the right woman to play the genteel but steely Scot was an Irishwoman—specifically, the profusely talented singer/actress Maria Doyle Kennedy. Known for her work in films like *The Commit-*

ments and *Sing Street*, and just off her television run on *Orphan Black*, Kennedy had an opening in her schedule that the *Outlander* team quickly pounced on to invite her to read for the show. She was unaware of the books or the series but says, "When I was told about Jocasta, everything about her was immediately compelling. She seems to be, in spirit, a woman completely displaced. She possessed a sort of a strength and tenacity and intellect that she would constantly have had to hide in those times, so that initially was really interesting."

Jocasta's blindness was also something new for Kennedy to play, and she was taken by how vividly it was described in the character breakdowns. "It said she can't see, but sometimes maybe some shadows of light, and she doesn't look as if she's blind," the actress remembers. "There was never going to be a situation where I could wear lenses, or any kind of covering of my eyes, so all of that was really interesting."

But the thing Kennedy says sold her on the role was playing Jocasta's unique loneliness and displacement. "Her formation is Scottish and now she's trying to navigate the colonial waters of Carolina," the actress muses about Jocasta. "She doesn't have an ability to meet and fraternize with like-minded women, which would be immediately what we would do now. She just never, at any stage, could do that. She couldn't even use her own language and customs and traditions all the time, because, again, she was in a new place. Then she lost her

children. She's been through three husbands. It's just the richest tapestry of adventure."

Kennedy says a lot of that comes through the first time we meet Jocasta, welcoming Jamie and Claire into her home in "Do No Harm." The actress imagined the realities of the time in terms of distance from family and the lack of instant communication to connect. "Your ideas and feelings for [your] people would only become magnified into a rosy-hued vision of home," she theorizes. "And again, the constant longing would cause you too much sadness and pain. So the fact that her sister's child is coming to see her, along with his wife, the more I thought about it, the more overwhelming I felt it would be. It would just be such a deeply moving thing for her to happen."

Yet Jocasta Cameron is also a wealthy landowner and a person of distinction in the very early days of the colonial class system. She's bought into all the trappings of society, and Kennedy says that's a source of instant conflict with Jamie and Claire. "She's the head of everything that happens around her, or at least that's the way she sees it," the actress says, smiling. "She's always thinking bigger picture, no matter how strong the smaller picture is. So, with Claire, it's so exciting to see a woman that is so strong and opinionated and so deeply bound to her husband. But Claire's views are so challenging to

her. I think it would have been easy for me as a person to try and tone Jocasta down a little bit and portray her like she really was against slavery. But that wasn't the truth of her. She says herself, 'Some of my best friends are slaves,' but there's no indication whatsoever that she thought there was anything fundamentally wrong with the system or that she tries in any way to change it. She accepted the hierarchical system and just found her own way to survive within that. That's a really deep, fundamental difference between her and Claire."

Kennedy admits she was just finding her feet with Jocasta as a recurring character in season four when it was time to let her go for the bulk of the season, as the narrative shifted. But she never saw the separation from the company as a disadvantage. "There's a kind of a power in being a new energy," she enthuses about when it was time to return to work. "It's not like they have to get to know you again. We've known each other, done some great work together, so we're on the level."

Kennedy also got to establish a relationship between Jocasta and Brianna, who essentially becomes her ward at River Run, as Jamie, Claire, and Ian go search for Roger. "From my observation of relationships between parents and their children, when they get a second go at it, they get to be more magical. They get to be a little bit kinder, or a little bit more creative, or a little bit more indulgent, and there's something about

that for me with Jocasta and Brianna," the actress explains. "Jocasta has lost all of her own children. And Jamie's the closest thing she's had to family ever. So to find this new person, and then for it to be another generation down, it's just like another go for her at having family and maybe doing better."

As Jocasta tries to find potential suitors for Bree, Kennedy says, it brings out a softer side of the woman. "It certainly brought out all the most loving aspects of Jocasta and a real desire to protect and almost to make up for her own failure as a parent with the things she did wrong and the children that she left behind in Scotland."

And it certainly softened Jocasta up for Murtagh, who ends up becoming her lover in the season finale. "Oh my God, what a goer," she laughs about the surprise reveal. "We're often led to believe that people over sixty-five don't exist as sexual beings, so I thought it was brilliant that they're going to go for that. I had thought it was going to be a different thing altogether, so when I read the script I was like, 'Okay.' But the way that it's written, you can understand that there's a magnetic force between them. They're so passionate, and they're very lonely. And they have a deep, deep understanding of the same things, of the same place, and of the same upbringing. I mean, they've known each other all their lives. So, the deep, deep connection people have can never be underestimated."

EPISODE 405: SAVAGES

WRITER: BRONWYN GARRITY DIRECTOR: DENISE DI NOVI

In "Savages," audiences are witness to the passage of time on Fraser's Ridge as Jamie and Claire's home is finished and warmly lived in. Since both are now comfortable in their environment, Jamie leaves Claire to try to enlist new tenants for their land, while Claire does her medical rounds with neighbors, including the Muellers and her Cherokee healer friends.

> *"Sam and I had this little scene where Jamie's getting ready to leave, and he's getting some jerky out of the jar. They just have this little dance that they do in this space that feels so familiar and you can see that there's a joy in the domesticity of it all."*
>
> —CAITRIONA BALFE

"Bronwyn was excited about this relationship that Claire had with Adawehi [Tantoo Cardinal], who in the book was Nayawenne," producer Shaina Fewell says of the episode's origins. "We loved Claire's relationship with that character so much that we really wanted to build a story around it. So a lot of where that story came from was, how can we get deeper into Claire's relationship with the Native Americans,

where she was learning so much about medicine from this woman. It's always great to have Claire have a friend who understands what she's going through."

Jamie also gets a friend—his best friend, in fact, with the surprise reveal of Murtagh as Wilmington's blacksmith. "Everyone loves Murtagh, so there were lots of pitches of how to bring him in," Fewell reveals. "He's such an exciting character to play with, because he does bring out a different dimension in Jamie. In this new land, Jamie has to be the man in charge, and so this is the one person that he can be a little bit

> "When they shot that reunion scene, where Murtagh's a blacksmith and Jamie is mad because Ian has given him all of their money, that was just one of those moments where everybody knew, 'Duncan, you're so powerful in this show.' He performed a 10 every take. You could just feel it. The same with Sam. These two characters that are so invested in each other, just seeing each other, there was so much energy in the room the day that we shot that scene."
>
> —SHAINA FEWELL

vulnerable with, in a way that we love.

"And [in the books], Diana had weaved in the Regulator movement and the War of [the] Regulation," Fewell continues. "It felt like a really interesting move to have Murtagh come into that. It's so natural. Of course he would be fighting the cause of the Regulators and be sympathetic to their concerns. And because Jamie just got this land, it would be the perfect thing, for the first time, to have something between them. So it's not just bringing him back but bringing him back with a real dilemma."

"We thought it was such a fun moment when [Murtagh] comes up to the Ridge. We had originally written in the script that he would be whistling the tune from season one, episode fourteen. Caitriona and Duncan loved it, so we kept it in and it worked so wonderfully."

—MARIL DAVIS

The woman who framed that momentous reunion is renowned producer-turned-director Denise Di Novi (*Batman Returns, Practical Magic*). "I had such a great time shooting his reveal, because his face is worth a million dollars," she enthuses about Lacroix. "There was real emotion and real chemistry between them. The actors are happy that Murtagh is back. Sam and Caitriona are happy, and to see the emotion on Sam's face when he realizes that it's Murtagh in the new land I think is such a powerful moment, and it was so rewarding to direct that."

However, back on the Ridge, the story turns very grave for Claire when the newborn child of their neighbors, the Muellers, dies from the measles. The father, Gerhard, blames the local Cherokee for cursing them and gets violent. Claire, left alone in the cabin, must defend herself. "I think Claire is a very underappreciated, unsung feminist heroine," Di Novi states. "She has incredible strength, integrity, and intelligence, so she was my touchstone in every scene, because I felt

"I am beyond a fanatic of the show, which I think some on the show thought was a little bit funny, because I knew every tiny detail about the characters, the setting, the book. I've read the books, each one twice at different points in my life, and they're up there with my favorite books. My husband, when I met him, had been reading the books because he's of Scottish descent, and that was one of the things I liked about him. To me, it was just a dream come true to be able to live in [the Outlander] world for a few months."

—DIRECTOR DENISE DI NOVI

"Burning down the Muellers' cabin was a similar approach to burning the printshop. It was slightly different because we did burn the cabin this time, as it was a set that we could burn down, but we couldn't do it in the woods. [VFX added] a lot more fire and made the continuity work. Using [footage] of the cabin in the woods, we added interactive lighting patterns and then just burning it stage by stage."

—VFX SUPERVISOR RICHARD BRISCOE

that she is always on the right side. Yet on the other hand she has tremendous compassion for everyone, so she understood the difficulties that the Muellers had and where they came from.

"Claire is a tough woman and she can protect herself to a certain degree, more so than most women in this time," the director continues. "Mr. Mueller's going through such a horrible experience, and Claire's stuck in the middle of it. Those moments, when she grabbed the gun and she was ready, she owned it. You believe it. And it's so wonderful to have a character that's strong, and you know she's gonna make choices that have been really thought out. I get excited about those moments because it's a very quiet story for Claire, because so much of the story takes place with her alone, waiting for possible danger."

Despite the horrific nature of the moment, Di Novi's favorite scene in the episode is when Gerhard comes to the house and gives Claire Adawehi's scalp. "It was so emotional shooting that," she shares. "I so appreciate that Matt and Toni included that in the episode and that they allowed the time to see how much pain this has caused Claire and how, with such reverence, she put the scalp in an honored place.

"With the level of tragedy with the German family, and the fire, and the Indians, that was very painful and very emotional for me," Di Novi admits. "And as an American working with Native Americans, it really brought it home for me, the history of native people in America and what occurred."

We got two of them because we thought, like with babies, that we'd probably have to use both of them. We named one Whiskey and then named the other one Mac Dubh, after Jamie's character, and we called him Dewey. We had an animal trainer that we use for all our animals, and he raised these puppies and was training them. Then we also got John Bell involved very early, just because you want to build that bond. It became very apparent pretty quickly that Dewey was more of an actor of the two, and they didn't look as alike as we'd hoped. Dewey is the least ferocious animal in the history of the planet. We had to adjust some of the dialogue in the scripts because of his menace and violence; we had to take that out. Sadly, in some of the episodes we have to add barks for him. But one of my favorite shots ever, you see Jamie and Claire and some of the Mohawks gliding by in these canoes and you just see Rollo sitting there. It's so adorable."

—MARIL DAVIS

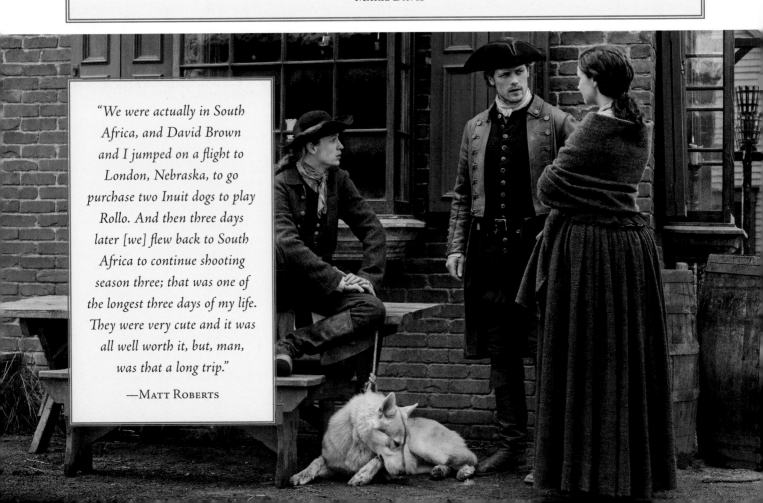

"We were actually in South Africa, and David Brown and I jumped on a flight to London, Nebraska, to go purchase two Inuit dogs to play Rollo. And then three days later [we] flew back to South Africa to continue shooting season three; that was one of the longest three days of my life. They were very cute and it was all well worth it, but, man, was that a long trip."

—MATT ROBERTS

"Rollo was so important because that relationship between Rollo and Young Ian in the book is to me so special. It's like Rollo intuitively just knows everything Young Ian is thinking and is such a protector. Certainly the most important animal in the series is Rollo. In the book, he's described as being this humongous dog and we were like, 'Where are we going to find one of those?'"

—MARIL DAVIS

"We were in season three and I said very early on that we need to start looking for [Rollo] because it's just the way it works. We're gonna need a wolf dog, and it's gotta be trained, and it's gotta be on set, and it's gotta be ready to be throughout the season. Now, the U.K. doesn't have the same animals as on the North American continent. Even the United States doesn't have the same animals they had two hundred fifty years ago, so that was a big challenge."

—MATT ROBERTS

SPOTLIGHT

DUNCAN LACROIX AS MURTAGH FITZGIBBONS FRASER

Per the canon of Diana Gabaldon's *Outlander* books, the arc of Murtagh FitzGibbons Fraser should have come to an end on the bloody battlefield of Culloden. Yet as is often the way when a book is adapted to screen, narratives and character destinies don't always follow the same paths. And so actor Duncan Lacroix's much-lauded character of Murtagh was spared the expected grim death in "The Battle Joined" and lived on to see many other days in seasons three and four of the *Outlander* series.

Over two seasons, Lacroix's role as Jamie's trusted kinsman and confidant thoroughly charmed both audiences and, more important, the series producers. Murtagh's stay of execution earned many a sigh of relief from the fandom and certainly from the actor playing him.

"I was made aware by [then executive producer] Ira Behr when we were filming season two that they wanted to keep the character alive going forward," Lacroix admits. "Nothing really official, though, and I really wasn't sure until I was offered an option for seasons going forward, which happened in the hiatus between season two and three."

While Lacroix's talents were secured, the answer to how often and why Murtagh might appear in future narratives was far vaguer. "I knew he'd survived the battle," the actor confirms, but otherwise he had to wait for the scripts to arrive to plan his performance decisions.

As it turns out, "All Debts Paid" became the episode that revealed Murtagh's survival, as tenuous as it was due to post-battle illness. Inside Ardsmuir prison, he and Jamie were able to have more of those heartfelt moments that audiences have come to savor between the two men. "They were some wonderful scenes," the actor shares. "And one didn't make it to the episode. It involved Jamie telling Murtagh he'd come back after escaping to look after him."

Murtagh was ultimately sold off to the Americas as an indentured servant with his fellow Scots, and his story was complete for season three. However, in the original scripting, Murtagh was set to show up in Jamaica.

"I was all set to go to South Africa with a couple of weeks to go," Lacroix remembers. "I had the work visa sorted but, at the last minute, the [producers] gave me a phone call to say the Murtagh story line had been dropped. The writers' room couldn't come up with a sufficient enough reason for him to be in Jamaica." Disappointed for sure, the actor says, but he quickly got on

with it afterward. "I think things ultimately worked out for the best, but I missed out on all the fun and sun," he laughs.

Lacroix says he was briefed by the producers that Murtagh would show up in the American colonies, but again he wasn't sure how, until he received the script for "Savages." In it, he discovered that Murtagh was now a blacksmith in Woolam's Creek but also leading a double life as a tax-protesting Regulator.

In preparation, the actor took up training with a blacksmith. "I had one two-hour session with him, where I made a pretty scrappy-looking knife out of a strip of steel and learned different techniques on how to hammer on different parts of the anvil," he enthuses. "The tools and the bellows we were using were all of the period, so it was fascinating."

The other core component of shaping this new version of Murtagh was figuring out how to demonstrate the eleven years of hard living he's done since Jamie, and the audience, last saw him in Ardsmuir prison. "We left it quite late for hair and makeup tests," he admits. "I had previously spoken with Maril [Davis] and Annie [McEwan], our makeup expert, about a Sam Elliott look, but the wig that arrived didn't have nearly enough gray in it. So we sent it back and the 'Gandalf' arrived," he jok-

ingly nicknames the final wig he wore. "It just seemed to work as soon as I put it on, and the 'Silver Fox' was born."

Once outward appearances were worked out, Lacroix says, the easy part was reuniting with Heughan and Balfe once more as his scene partners. "I've come to really care about those two as people over the years since we started," he offers. "I really can't sing their praises enough both as actors and people. There was always something very natural, comfortable, and rhythmic about any scene I had with either of them, and we picked up exactly where we left off."

Yet there was one thing about Murtagh's return to the series that Lacroix admits made him uneasy: the fan reaction to such a deep departure from Gabaldon's canon. Having shot his scenes months in advance, he had to keep his return secret and then wait until "Savages" aired in December of 2018 to see how it would all play out.

At the time, the actor reveals, he was on a camper holiday in New Zealand, so he could only peek at the reactions when he managed to get Wi-Fi coverage. But when he did, a weight was lifted. "The blacksmith scene where Murtagh and Jamie reunite seemed to hit just the right spot with most of the fans. The majority of the comments were very heartwarming."

As season four progressed, Lacroix was happy to explore new facets of his character, as a reinvigorated rabble-rouser. "Anger is definitely a large part of his palette now," the actor agrees. "He still has a tender and loving side, which we see whenever he is around family, but he is driven by a sense of injustice and resentment now. That darker side of his character has always been there. It's a grim and bleak sense of determination that now consumes him at the core. I try not to let it become too vociferous or showy but let it inform his demeanor as an undertone."

Murtagh's new cause also creates a huge problem for Jamie, which will have repercussions into future seasons. Lacroix says the clash of ideology and family will force him to have to make unexpected choices. "He is a man who for a long period of time lost everything that was dear to him, even his identity as a Highlander. Rather than crumble, he has hammered his anger and resentment into a cold hard belief in a cause. He has replaced his clan of Highlanders with a clan of Regulators. He has replaced his loyalty and fidelity to Jamie and family to loyalty and fidelity to the rights of his new kinsmen. Now [that] he has his family back, there are huge decisions ahead for him."

EPISODE 406: BLOOD OF MY BLOOD

WRITER: SHAINA FEWELL DIRECTOR: DENISE DI NOVI

In "Blood of My Blood," two very important people from Jamie's past show up at Fraser's Ridge: Lord John Grey and Jamie's son, William. An emotional exploration of love and unexpected family, the episode was one that immediately appealed to producer/writer Shaina Fewell. "It was one of those episodes that we all knew was going to be quieter, but the story line between John Grey and Claire, I was just in love with that stuff in the book. No one is really accepting of who he is in this time, and that part of the book just popped to me in such a powerful way. I was so excited to dig into that and play that out."

Director Denise Di Novi was also thrilled to frame an episode around one of her favorite book characters. "Lord John Grey is such a poignant character, and I find his love for Jamie so heartbreaking. He gives Jamie an opportunity to illuminate how deep his goodness and compassion is, because Jamie knows how much Lord John Grey loves him, and he accepts it, and he

gives it a dignity that I find very moving."

Fewell flew to Scotland for the first time to produce her episode in person and deeply appreciated Di Novi's approach of letting the two parallel story lines—Jamie and Willie, and Claire and John—play out as linearly as possible. "Denise leaned in and found really wonderful ways to tell those stories," she enthuses. "It really was one of those things where the stars were aligned. People just came together on it, and understood, and really fought for the moments to be able to happen, and gave the actors the free-

"Denise was so incredible. You could really feel that when she came onto the set she had all these great ideas, and she came at it from a place of 'Oh, I love when Jamie and Claire do this.' And not to say that our other directors aren't as knowledgeable, but I don't know that all of them come to the show as such fans as well. It was great to be able to create that stuff with her and with Sam."

—CAITRIONA BALFE

dom to breathe and dig in. And they did."

Di Novi helped cast Oliver Finnegan as the older William. "I wanted it to feel that he was believable as Jamie's son at this later age, but he also had to be believable as a boy who had been raised as an aristocrat," she explains. "I think he understood, on a deep level, what this story was really about.

"And it was fun for Sam to experience being a fatherly character," she continues. "By the end of the episode, he really enjoyed it, and it followed the course of the story in that he didn't know Oliver at the

"[Oliver] is a young, very talented boy. It was about trying to build some sort of relationship between us as actors. So it was fun to find his humor and to make him at ease but also to make myself feel at ease. I don't have much experience with children. It was all new to me as well, and it was great. You get to see that there's a bond between these two people. Like that moment when William saves Jamie with the Native Americans by offering himself, that was a really strong moment. You see Jamie fill with pride for his son."

—SAM HEUGHAN

beginning and by the end of the episode they were quite close." Di Novi knows that bond helped sell the emotion of father and son parting once more. "For Jamie to have this little window of time to be a father and to know that his son will now remember him—I get choked up talking about it. And the most important thing to me was that moment where his son turns his head and looks back at him. There were a lot of alternatives, and I just wanted it to be perfect, because when [Willie] said to him, 'You never looked at me, you never came back,' now he turns and looks at him, and I think it tells Jamie, and

the audience, that Willie does love him and he will see him again."

Meanwhile, the scenes with Claire desperately trying to save John from the measles were just as intimate and revealing, as they get very honest with each other about their love for Jamie. "Caitriona and I spoke about it a lot," Di Novi says of how they found the right tone for Claire's reactions to John. "I think she's jealous of all the years that John had with Jamie that she lost. And in a way, [Jamie and John] had a child together, and she was not able to have Brianna with Jamie. I found that such a rich thing to explore."

With the duo relegated to the cabin set, Di Novi says it was "like two heavyweights going into the ring. They played off of each other so incredibly. And I wanted it to be believable that he was actually dying, because when I watch scenes

where people are supposed to be on their deathbed and they're just chatting away normally, it feels fake to me. So keeping that, as well as getting the performance and the dialogue correct, was very difficult."

"The scene where he says, 'So do I,' that moment killed everyone on set every time, because you could just feel that they were so committed in those moments," Fewell says with deep praise. "You feel so much for him in a way because we all love Jamie and Claire together, and here's this person who's an interruption on a certain level. But what really ends up happening is that he bonds with Jamie on a level that no one else can, and he bonds with Claire on a level that no one else can. I just found their relationships to be so fascinating."

After all of Claire's and Jamie's separate emotional heavy lifting, they get to come together in a very romantic moment. "I really wanted

> "I decided that I would write letters to Sam, as John, to fill in that time to flesh out what had been going on between John and Jamie in that interim between Jamaica and North Carolina."
>
> —DAVID BERRY ON
> HIS BACKSTORY WORK
> BETWEEN SEASONS

to end the show on a scene that showed them settling back into their relationship and this domestic relationship that they have now forged," Di Novi says. "I wanted to end the episode seeing them together in this very beautiful, intimate moment of him bathing her and giving her the ring, bringing everything back to them. I loved the last few moments, because I also wanted to show the humor and the sweetness when they're counting the kisses. They're relaxed in their lives together now."

> "David Berry is so fun to work with. He really challenges me when I'm on set. He definitely likes to push the boundary sometimes and see if there's new things that we can discover in that relationship. There wasn't a lot in season four for us, so we really had to work with each moment. I think that there's a great humor as well between the two of them."
>
> —SAM HEUGHAN

BUILDING SEASON FOUR: COSTUMES

As is always the case with *Outlander*, the new season ushered in a narrative in a brand-new land, the Americas, featuring settlers from all over Europe and indigenous Native Americans. That meant a whole new array of costumes to research and create from scratch. As far back as season three, costume designer Terry Dresbach anticipated the mountain of work they would face with the *Drums of Autumn* adaptation. "I'm the one leaping up and down in the air like Paul Revere waving the bell, going, 'This is coming! This is coming! We have to figure this out,'" she laughs. "Everybody is looking at you, going, 'We just started shooting season three. Will you *shut up* about season four?' Fortunately, with season two, I'd earned enough trust from everybody that maybe they should listen."

As a fan and devotee of interpreting Gabaldon's text into reality,

Dresbach knew Native Americans would play a big part in the Frasers' lives, so she started her research on Eastern Woodland Indians about a year in advance of shooting. Initially her research was on the Tuscarora but then shifted to the Cherokee. "I'm lucky—whereas Gary [Steele] has to wait for scripts, I don't really have to," she explains. "All I need is a number, right? What's the maximum number of Native Americans we're going to see? Two hundred? Then I can go from there."

Dresbach says the process of trying to be historically accurate with the Cherokee and then the Mohawk costumes was daunting. "You are talking about the people who inhabited a region that had been completely wiped out. I have an extensive library now on the Indians of America, but it's still all interpretation. What is out there is an interpretation, usually by white people. The Smithsonian even said to me, 'Well, there just isn't a lot. What information there was burned in the Civil War.' So at a certain point you have to go, 'There's no more research to do.'

"I keep saying you build the puzzle," she continues. "There's a bunch of missing pieces, so you have to use your heart and your brain and your logic, common sense, and experience to fill in the missing pieces. As Ron is always saying, 'People can glean a truth from it.' That was the goal and that's what we did, and I think we did it successfully."

The other big issue to tackle was making costumes for the appropriate season. Shooting Scotland for the colonies meant the cast and extras were still going to be working in an environment with dramatic weather. "If we were going to shoot a North Carolina summer when it's winter in Scotland, and I'm putting everybody in clothes for hot weather and then spraying them with water to look like they were sweating, [we're] gonna end up with a lot of sick people," Dresbach explains pragmatically. "So the decision was made that we would shoot according to the season that we were actually in in Scotland. That saved us. It meant that I didn't have to rebuild the Europeans to summer in America, as that would have been absolutely impossible. We wouldn't have had the time, money, or anything else to do that."

Knowing their parameters for the season, there was still a large amount of work to complete, so co-costume designer Nina Ayres moved into the Glasgow offices to help split the workload with

> *"Most people were dressed underneath their costumes. They would have had thermals on. Even if they wore cotton or linen skirts, a woman could have like three of them on and once you've got those layers, you're covered. We were obviously always taking that into consideration that nobody would freeze to death. We just had tons and tons of thermals so everybody was packed out. Everyone's looking slightly fatter than they actually are."*
>
> —NINA AYRES

"With every costume that you
see in seasons three and four,
everything will either circle back
to an earlier part of that
character's life or earlier to
another's life. So Fergus connects
to Jamie, and Marsali connects
to her mother and to Claire.
And Brianna to her mother
and her father. You just start
drawing these lines, and it was a
very rich experience."

—TERRY DRESBACH

Dresbach and her costuming team. "Terry had done a lot of research on fabric choices, as the clothes transition to a lot of pattern and linen and various cottons," Ayres explains. "It was similar to what had happened in the Jamaica [sequences], where there was that little transition of fabric choices and we're trying to recycle all the [costume] stock from Scotland. We started repurposing and dyeing everything to get a fresh feel for the stock. So many

hundreds of thousands of things are needed for every extra, and we started with the Wilmington scene. On day one, there were about two hundred extras."

In her research, Ayres looked for ways to repurpose the British redcoat uniforms from the Battle of Culloden in season three for the settlers in the colonies. "What could we do to the red coats to make them look different? We had hundreds of them. I had to think of a solution, without putting another order in to another company for another hundred coats. It was what could we do with the preexisting ones to bring them up to date and make them look like they live in colonial America."

She continues, "And I was looking at European settlers and had loads and loads of research for Germany and Spain and Denmark, all the different places that these people would have come from to settle. Rather than dressing somebody in a fake Danish costume, I just brought in elements of their

pattern and their embroidery or their hat shape. I spent quite a lot of time getting some different hats made so that it was bringing those European influences in. It was like this big melting pot of different patterns and a bolder color palette as well."

When it came to costuming the main and recurring cast, Dresbach continued to dress and fit Cait, Sam, and Sophie. Ayres took responsibility for Ed Speleers, Richard Rankin, Duncan Lacroix, and

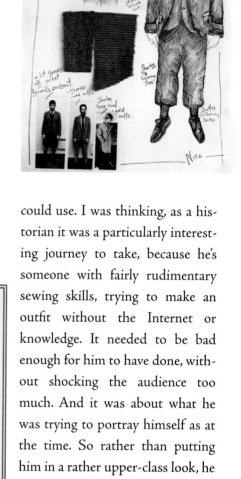

good quality. His coat would actually stop the rain; his boots practically do what he wants [them] to do. It was that and the silhouette of him, and the way his coat swished."

⚜ Roger Wakefield

"I had to use preexisting costumes that he had, that he would have done a very bad job making into a costume to go through the stones. Everything he wears is a remake of something he's worn before. Even the stock around his neck was a shirt he had worn before. It was challenging to pick which items of clothes that he possessed that he

Maria Doyle Kennedy. For each, she explains her overall aesthetic for the character:

⚜ Stephen Bonnet

"I was quite surprised by the casting of this. There were gruesome pirate types that I had envisioned, but Ed's got quite a cute, soft face. I thought that was absolutely pleasant, and therefore, with his costume, I didn't make it villainous in any way, shape, or form. I purposely chose lighter colors and a bit of patterns. He starts off in the season how he ends the season. He starts off down on his luck at the prison, then he has a pretty good time in the middle, then he ends the season back in jail. It's full circle, which I thought was really nice. He wears what he can actually pick up on his travels, so his outfit doesn't particularly come together. It's just pieces of clothing which seem alike, and they're fairly

"We gave Brianna the Gunne Sax dress, as if she went into her closet and said, 'Oh sure, why not?' The way we saved it from being totally ludicrous was that she's smart enough to know that it can't be short. So she puts a long petticoat underneath it. The other thing she gets out of her closet is the cape that I had in 1970, a floor-length tweed cape.

By wearing that, she covers enough of that costume to get her through to a place where we can change her clothes and put her in her mother's clothes, which is what we ended up doing."

—Terry Dresbach on Brianna's clothing choices to go through the stones

could use. I was thinking, as a historian it was a particularly interesting journey to take, because he's someone with fairly rudimentary sewing skills, trying to make an outfit without the Internet or knowledge. It needed to be bad enough for him to have done, without shocking the audience too much. And it was about what he was trying to portray himself as at the time. So rather than putting him in a rather upper-class look, he knew he would be taking a ship to the Americas. He would have chosen a look that doesn't make him look suspicious as a crew member. I went for a more sailor look for him. I had to make patterns of his preexisting outfits and work out in the simplest way how we would turn it into a more eighteenth-century jacket shape. Even the bubble hat—he cuts it off and pulls it down to become a sailor cap from the eighteenth century."

disguise all the time, but the kilt is his real attire. The patchwork trousers are practical as he is not a rich person. He also doesn't want to stand out. It was a mix-and-match wardrobe, which was for everyone. It looks less like Scotland and is more of a hodgepodge with cottons and prints."

Jocasta Cameron

"She stands alone in time and is very much wearing nice clothing. Everyone else in America is descaled. Knowing that nobody was particularly wealthy, except for Jocasta, it was more about her living in a total bubble. It was all about patterns and everything imported from Europe. It was like power dressing and putting up this front. But we changed her a bit toward the end. She's out of date with her fashion but she relaxes her formidable style. It was purposeful to make her look more motherly and show a softer side to her."

Chief Tehwahsehkwe

"It was an absolutely huge, huge amount of research, and really just being a Mohawk chief, there's just so much to tell about it. There's the lovely and special way that he wears that beautiful duster all the time. I wanted to show a difference between the Mohawk and the Cherokee. We decided the Mohawk might have had more wampum

Murtagh Fraser

"A lot of it was talking to Duncan. He's very practical and loved the idea of the piece of tartan from Ardsmuir prison. So the secret part of him is the brooch with the piece of tartan on the chest of his waistcoat. And then I made the decision for him not to wear his kilt unless he was going to meetings. He's in

than the Cherokee, or the Mohawk had more metalwork. And the Mohawk was more geometric, and the Cherokee was softer with fluid lines. We had bolder colors with the Mohawk and the softer colors of the Cherokee. We really did try hard to get the research right and make every craft piece completely beautifully and honor their culture."

EPISODE 407: DOWN THE RABBIT HOLE

WRITER: SHANNON GOSS DIRECTOR: JENNIFER GETZINGER

When Brianna sees a newspaper obituary for the deaths of Jamie and Claire in the late 1700s, she decides to travel through the stones, and back in time, to personally warn them of their fate. "Down the Rabbit Hole" not only tests her mettle two hundred years in the past but also forces her to reconcile

her feelings about her father Frank and meeting Jamie.

"We always knew we wanted to do a Frank episode," executive producer Toni Graphia reveals. "In the book, we don't see what happens after Frank leaves the house and gets in the car wreck. We always keyed on the fact that Frank was bragging to Claire, 'Our daughter will come

"Bree almost has this ironic
giggle to herself at the people
of the time. Like when she has
that scene with Laoghaire, and
Laoghaire's saying, 'Oh, that
woman bewitched my husband!'
Bree reacts like, 'I'm sympathetic
to you, but that's actually quite
ridiculous,' but she can't say
anything. Things like that
are always fun to play."

—SOPHIE SKELTON

with me when I go to London.' We came up with the idea to see what happens if he went and found Brianna and she says no because she's so upset. It's a scar on her heart that she wears, and it's a guilty secret that she beats herself up about. She never told her mom, and we always knew we wanted to show that."

Brianna's travels in Scotland end up unknowingly connecting her with Laoghaire, in a situation that allows audiences to see another side of the woman they love to hate. "We knew the fans might be a little trepidatious about a Laoghaire story, but we thought it was an interesting pair to put together." Graphia smiles. "She's staying with Laoghaire, and neither one knows who [the] other is, which is very juicy. And we thought this would maybe soften Laoghaire a bit. She's a lot of things, but she's a good mom. Marsali is awesome, and strong, and spirited. And Joan is sweet. She provides for them. A lot of people don't like Frank, but he's a good dad too. We thought there's a really cool parallel here between Frank and Laoghaire, because both of them are the outsiders."

Returning to direct this epi-

"We had a little hiccup with
Brianna going to Lallybroch
and not being able to get Laura
Donnelly [Jenny] at the last
minute, which really threw us.
We love Laura Donnelly and
love the character of Jenny, but
obviously we had to at the last
minute go back and rewrite that
episode. And, actually, it turned
out to be one of my favorite
episodes of the season, in terms
of the Laoghaire story."

—MARIL DAVIS

sode was Jennifer Getzinger, who'd also directed season-three episodes featuring Frank and Laoghaire. "I asked, 'Did you guys do this on purpose?' but it happened by chance," she explains. "But I got Tobias and Nell back!"

Getzinger says she loved being able to have Brianna chase the ghosts of her parents in the episode. "I shot Lallybroch before, so I knew the beauty angles and did similar framing to get across the idea of Brianna retracing Claire's steps. Even when we did the drive up to Lallybroch, as they're riding up in the wagon, we did that from over Sophie's shoulders so that you really felt like you were approaching it with her."

In the flashbacks where Bree thinks about Frank, Graphia says, they talked about her feeling disloyal as she inches closer to Jamie in America. "We love the irony that

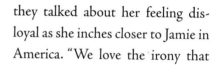

"I'd never worked with Ed [Speleers] before, but we were immediately on the same page with how we work. We had very common objectives in the scene. We had very limited time to build a relationship between Roger and Bonnet, but we were immediately fascinated by the relationship between the two. It was one of my favorite parts of season four, working with Ed. The scenes are great, but it wasn't even just necessarily the content of the scene. Sometimes it's just about being there with that other actor and affecting each other, listening, provoking. I feel like we played that. We really listened to each other. It was no rehearsed reaction."

—RICHARD RANKIN

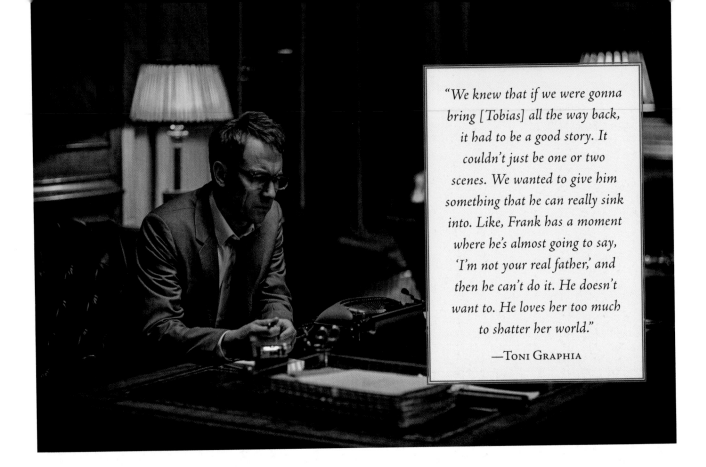

"We knew that if we were gonna bring [Tobias] all the way back, it had to be a good story. It couldn't just be one or two scenes. We wanted to give him something that he can really sink into. Like, Frank has a moment where he's almost going to say, 'I'm not your real father,' and then he can't do it. He doesn't want to. He loves her too much to shatter her world."

—TONI GRAPHIA

the most she's thinking about Frank is when she's in Scotland, because it's letting go," the writer points out. "It's a goodbye to the father that raised her yet an acknowledgment that he'll always be with her."

"I loved the ending where she has that vision of [Frank]," Getzinger effuses. "It was completely raining that day, and rain is a funny thing. Unless it's really, really heavy, you can't read it on camera. Tobias was actually getting pretty drenched as we just tried so many different ways of him waving goodbye. When we got to the one that we ended up using, he knew that was it. We all knew. It was just them looking across this sea of people and then really feeling a connection between them for that last moment."

The episode also tracked Rog-

er's harrowing experiences as a seaman for Stephen Bonnet. "I thought that Roger and Bonnet had a great rapport with each other," Getzinger

"It is always about returning, and repeating, and making those connections. When I was able to put Brianna back in that coat and green plaid dress that Claire wears in season one, hopefully it touches people in the really visceral way that you try to do when you're telling stories with clothes. Somebody said to me the other day, 'I'm a writer, and you've taught me how to tell stories without words.'"

—TERRY DRESBACH ON THE
MOTHER–DAUGHTER CLOTHING
CONNECTION

says admiringly. In particular, the scene where Bonnet throws the sick child overboard was intense. "We just all kept saying, 'God, I can't believe we have to do this,'" she remembers. "Just the thought of what we were even suggesting was awful. We did do it a few times and at one point, unexpectedly, Richard ran right up to the window that she'd been thrown out of, almost trying to grab her. I loved that he did that, so we put a camera outside the ship looking back in so we could really get him rushing right toward us."

With so many emotional beats covered in just one episode, Graphia assesses, "It's one of my favorites. It's way different than the book, but it's the most creative and out-of-the-box one we did this season."

SPOTLIGHT

ED SPELEERS AS STEPHEN BONNET

In the strange world of casting, sometimes an actor's greatest compliment is getting feedback that they would be a perfect psychopath. Such was the case for British actor Ed Speleers, known globally for his role as Jimmy Kent in *Downton Abbey*, who had gone in to audition for several roles on *Outlander* prior to his call to come in for season four.

Speleers remembers his agent saying to him, "They really wanna see if you're this Stephen Bonnet character. I read it and was like, 'He's Irish. I can't do Irish . . . and he's a psychopath!'" The pitch that actually intrigued him was the note that the producers wanted Bonnet to have the traits of real-life serial killer Ted Bundy, possessing charm and wit, "so

you don't see him coming," which sealed Speleers's interest.

"It felt like a no-brainer," he explains. "This is somebody I've not had a chance to play before and the sort of role that I've been crying out to play for a long time. He was someone where I could flex some muscles, challenge myself, and actually get over those hurdles of 'Can you convey this kind of character? You've been crying out to show someone with depth—can you actually deliver that?'

"I also love working in Scotland, so there was a big pull to go up there again and join this juggernaut of a show," he says, smiling. "It just felt like the right time for me to get back into a big show again, and this was definitely the part. The complexity of him drew me in quite early on."

As with any actor embodying a "villain," it's all about finding their character's point of view so they don't come off as one-note. For Speleers, he never felt he had to justify Bonnet's actions; rather, it was about understanding why. "There was no way I could take on something like this for it to be the archetypal villainous character. You need to understand how this person moves, why this person is, and he's always trying to think what he can get out of it. Whether it's because of his upbringing or lack of upbringing, it's that argument of nature versus nurture, which comes up time and time

again, in particular with these sorts of troubled characters," he muses, discussing what impacted Bonnet most. "It's given us as many layers as possible, and I think that's what you want."

Speleers also leaned deeply on Bonnet's abiding belief in luck. "That comes up in the series and in the books, that his faith is in the god of luck, Danu. So he makes a lot of his decisions based on the flip of a coin. The reason he's behind Danu is luck, which has presented me this opportunity where I can take advantage of someone. Luck has presented me this opportunity where I will get away from the hangman's noose."

Luck has also brought various members of the Fraser family across his path, which some might argue is more fate. Speleers thinks Bonnet wouldn't spend much time parsing the difference. "Whether he's bewildered by it, I almost don't think he's bothered by it. I get the impression that he wakes up in the morning and what will be today will be today."

As far as how Speleers wanted Bonnet to look, he admits he was inspired by the book's description of him. "The beauty of taking a character that's so well described in a book allows you to go, 'Oh, that's really good, I like that,' and you can magpie that. He was based on a guy called Stede Bonnet, who was a gentleman who then became a pirate. He was known as the pirate gentleman. I think Diana actually cultivated Ste-

phen Bonnet to be a loose relative of his, to play on this idea of his garments, his costume, his jewelry, to be really into the finer things in life. He took pride in his appearance, not necessarily the highest quality in terms of the finest, richest things from France and Italy but just very well cut, well crafted, but also practical. Like, I got a big heavy wax coat. He's also covered in rings. I don't know whether they were conquests, which could be quite a gruesome idea, or whether it's just that he's drawn to gold and wealth and riches.

"Now, there's obviously a caveat with that," the actor continues. "Actually, having all that might make him look a bit cheap, and if he was a classy gentleman, would he be covered in all this gold? Probably not. So he's that guy who is trying to play up himself and go one step beyond his station. He's got a point to prove. He feels like he's been outcast, downtrodden. So he's trying to wear the best clothes that he can, cover himself in diamonds and rubies and pearls in order to show 'I am worthy,' and I think that's quite interesting."

When Speleers looked in the mirror with final costume and makeup set, "I was really impressed with what the makeup department did. In the book, it describes him having this scar down his mouth. We didn't do the mouth, but we did add the scar, and I actually felt that it's a particularly interesting thing to add. It was not necessarily to make him look hard, but it tells a story."

With the appearance and psychology established, Speleers says, his first day of shooting was the first scene where audiences meet Bonnet. "I think the entrance for me did set the tone. It was a great way to fit in the skin, I suppose," he says. "We had the town, we had the hangman's noose, we had a drumbeat going on. It felt like we were going to watch a hanging, so it lent itself to get into character. That whole episode was shot in chronological order, which meant it was a nice little crescendo to the moment that's right at the end of the episode, which is good and quite rare as well."

While Bonnet's appearances are judiciously interspersed across season four, Speleers feels "Down the Rabbit Hole" is one of the best at truly revealing his character's worldview. When he is ready to throw sick children overboard to save everyone else's lives, it's pragmatism at its purest. "When playing someone like that, you have to get on board with who they are and what they're thinking," he explains. "I would say that the logic applied [there] is bang on. We're talking a time where decisions like that had to be made very quickly. Would I do that myself? Probably not, but actually what is the alternative? To harbor someone who is ill and let that spread across everybody on the ship? I'd say he made the right decision. Now, that doesn't mean that morally he always makes the right decisions, and maybe there was a better way of handling that, but I think it's quick, sharp. And it would be interesting having to battle with those morals. But also, when someone has a clear picture of 'this is what's gonna benefit me right now,' you open your eyes a bit to how people can be so unabashed."

EPISODE 408: WILMINGTON

WRITER: LUKE SCHELHAAS DIRECTOR: JENNIFER GETZINGER

A densely packed episode that sets the stage for the upcoming family reunion, "Wilmington" runs the gamut of emotions, featuring some of the season's highest highs and lowest lows, especially for Brianna and Roger. "We condensed a number of sections from the book and things that were in two different locations, and we put them into one, until we had everybody in the town of Wilmington," co–executive producer/writer Luke Schelhaas explains of the story connections. "The title 'Wilmington' was a bit of a nod to that. Then a whole bunch of things do happen, some of which are beautiful and some of which are horrible."

For fans of Brianna and Roger's complicated romance, the episode pays off with them finding each other and consummating their re-

lationship. Schelhaas says, "We wanted this to stand out as a series of scenes: the meeting, what is essentially the proposal, accepting the proposal, the handfasting, the lovemaking, and then the afterglow.

"And we wanted it to be beautiful and pure and tender and loving and true," he continues. "All these good words, and all these good ideas about what sex can be, what a marriage can be, and what a partnership can be."

Getzinger says the handfasting scene really lands the best of their relationship, and they adjusted de-

> "There's a moment where someone stumbles on Bree's shoes and then sets them aside. In the book, Bree actually escapes, and Bonnet's crew out in the ship [where she's assaulted], they catch her and return her to Bonnet. So this was our nod to that story element as well, that other people were complicit in this."
>
> —LUKE SCHELHAAS

tails to get it just right. "Originally it was written as a day scene, and I asked if it could be night. I also asked the production designer to put a fireplace in there so that we could make it feel more like a ceremony. We were able to shoot it in a way and have them perform it in a way that lent a great amount of respect to it."

Next came their "wedding night," which was new territory for the characters and the actors, so Getzinger was particularly sensitive to Sophie and Richard's comfort. "We actually did quite a bit of rehearsal ahead of time for those romantic scenes, figuring out beat by beat how they would move," she details. "It was a new thing for the actors, but I think the nervousness that they had worked out pretty well for the characters. We kept it a very safe environment for them, where it was only essential personnel, and on set it was deeply quiet and calm to let them really play the scene. I think it worked really well, as far as seeing that this is some-

thing [the characters] both had been wanting for a long time.

"But then it was interesting how the tone obviously shifts with Brianna's fight with Roger," the director points out. "We really rehearsed that a lot, just to try to keep it real and to try to really understand what makes her so angry about this. You realize that she just put all of her trust in this man and then realized that maybe she made a mistake."

In the aftermath of the fight, they separate, which puts Brianna in the path and clutches of Stephen Bonnet. Brianna's subsequent rape also occurs in the book and ignites a series of events integral to Gabaldon's narrative. Schelhaas says the writers' room debated including the story line at all because of how it had been used in previous seasons, as well as the current television climate in regard to the subject. "Not doing it really didn't seem like an option for us in terms of unraveling, honestly, everybody's story. So then it was, what is the best

"*Murtagh waiting in the woods didn't seem connected to what was going on, and we talked about that a lot. It was interesting because you did have to show these different things going on and connect them in a way that was subtle. Like there's a moment after Claire meets George Washington where she says, 'Brianna would've loved this,' and then we go to Brianna.*"

—Director Jennifer Getzinger on the tricky balance of the episode's stories

way to do this? We approach it from a point of view of story, but we also approach it from the point of view of being responsible toward people who are going to be viewing this.

"In the book, the rape plays as a flashback in a story told much later," he explains. "We put that in this episode because we told the story in actual time. We felt like we had to play it in the episode we chose to put it in. Then we made a very concerted decision to play it almost entirely offscreen. We played it on the reactions of the people who know this is going on and who do noth-

"*I discovered a play that was a period play called* The Prince of Parthia. *The play you see in the episode is a real play that was written by a man in Wilmington just a few years prior to the date of our episode. It is the first play written by a colonial American and produced in the colonies. As far as production goes, we actually hired a play director to work with the actors who were seen onstage to direct it as a play.*"

—Luke Schelhaas

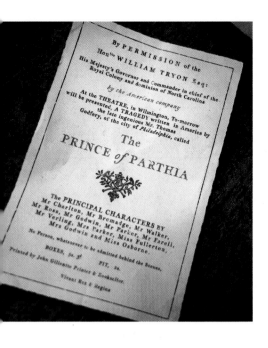

ing. We thought that was realistic for the times. It still plays horribly, because you see the front part of the attack."

In shooting the scene, Getzinger says, "I kept really checking in with Sophie and making sure she was okay. They let us just play at least a couple of beats of it, mostly the struggle, and I think it helped her to feel more scared. I love that she got to the place where she did at the end of it, because I also feel like once you decide that you're gonna show rape, you have to really show the reality of it. The compromise we did was to not show the exact act, but you still see that intense look on her face afterward, so you really know what happened. You have to see the real ramifications of what just happened."

> "Stephen Bonnet probably was a serial offender of [rape]. I think that they're not aware that they're being a serial offender of something as grave as this, and that's how I had to start getting my head around it. I had to try and see it as though that wasn't what was taking place. Because someone who's committing a crime like that, I don't think they view it that way. So I think that allowed it to be even more harrowing, because it's saying there is no problem here. This is just life; this is normal."
>
> —ED SPELEERS

BUILDING SEASON FOUR: VISUAL EFFECTS

I n a first for *Outlander* as a series, when the production crew started principal photography on season four, work was still being done on season three. In particular, the huge storm for the season-three finale, "Eye of the Storm," was in the throes of visual-effects completion.

Visual-effects supervisor Rich-ard Briscoe explains: "For the first two episodes, I was still literally working on the storm sequence while also covering what they're shooting in the Wilmington [sets]. I brought in another supervisor just to cover the shoots while I was busy finishing the storm. But in VFX, it's generally nose to the grindstone; you just get on with it."

As in every season, each plot and location brings with it a specific set of challenges that VFX often helps solve. With the Frasers now settling in colonial America, visual effects were needed to assist the country of Scotland in credibly standing in for the early days of North Carolina. Briscoe says he and his team leaned on many of the

ages with drones and did the same in a bunch of other places, so some of the waterfalls come from one place, the bend in the river comes from somewhere else, and the main hills come from somewhere else. The big hill in the distance, which actually looks very similar to the real Grandfather Mountain, was pure coincidence. The bulk of that image is one place, with a few enhancements dropped in, but it's essentially all filmed and not done as a matte painting."

lessons they had learned in prior seasons.

Fraser's Ridge

"The biggest problem [with Fraser's Ridge] is everyone has an idea of what it looks like. It's described not just in the books but in the dialogue and in the story onscreen. The description is it's the most amazing place you've ever seen, so you're kind of setting yourself up to fail on one level. It was problematical with the scheduling of [production] and the seasons. We couldn't necessarily shoot what should be out there at the time that we shot Jamie and Claire standing on the edge. Where we found good vistas, we couldn't get a [camera] unit up to put them on that edge. But we found areas actually very close to where we shot the Indian village, where we had views over a large valley. We shot a series of tiled im-

River Run

"[Production designer] Gary Steele did a great job of building a façade and veranda as far as they could, but the [shot of River Run] is a massive cheat. If you stand there—the space amongst those trees—there isn't the room for what we put in [the frame]. For example, with the main central façade, what we ended up doing down the line in post was give the building wings,

left and right, because we felt it was too small. As well as the upper floor and the roof and so on and so on. That's my favorite VFX out of the season, because it's invisible and people don't know. The [artists] who did it did it incredibly well, because actually putting that building behind all those thousands of branches and leaves takes a lot of work. There's real beauty to it."

Car Tricks

"When Brianna and Roger are driving on the way to the [Scottish festival], that was on a stage in the car. We shot some [footage] plates on some forested roads in Slovakia. I should point out that at least the first two or three times we see that car when it's driving in the urban environment from outside, that's a digital car. When it's driving across the bridge or when it's in traffic, that's a digital car."

The Death of Father Alexandre Ferigault

"It was challenging because we didn't have that much time [to complete VFX] at that point in the season. For all of the shots of the body on fire, we did it with dummies. We also shot the actors in the same position, so we blended them back into the fire. But we also created the simple things like all the close-ups of the priest. We had to make his clothing wet with sweat, and we had to put sweat all over his face. We were adding heat haze because when we shoot it, again, we can't actually put the actor that close to the flames."

EPISODE 409: THE BIRDS AND THE BEES

WRITERS: MATTHEW B. ROBERTS AND TONI GRAPHIA

DIRECTOR: DAVID MOORE

Just as fans were beside themselves in anticipation of Jamie and Claire's reunion in season three, so too were they excited about Jamie potentially meeting his daughter back in time. "The Birds and The Bees" made that moment

> *"I seem to remember a lot of giggling and trying to avoid eating too much of the cold food that was offered up. Yes, a lot of giggling."*
>
> —DUNCAN LACROIX ABOUT THE FRASER FAMILY DINNER SCENE

come true, while also playing out the sobering repercussions of Brianna's rape.

After his adept handling of two emotion-heavy episodes in season three, director David Moore returned to handle the Fraser family

"In the book [before they meet], Jamie's having a pee up against a tree. We did create a model which had a tree in the middle of it, then decided that a tree in the middle of our Wilmington just didn't make any sense at all."

—DAVID MOORE

reunion. However, Moore first had to open the episode directly from where "Wilmington" left off. "One of the first scenes is where Brianna comes back to the room, has to clean herself up and try not to give away [to her maid] what's hap-

pened to her. Sophie and myself decided that we would shoot it as simply and honestly as we could, which meant Sophie had the chance to just take her time over the performance, as they were all long takes. They were all difficult emotionally for her and we just, fully throughout the day, went through it. It was pretty brutal, pretty honest, and quite emotional," he says somberly.

But not long after in the narrative, Brianna's world is turned upside down when she finally meets Jamie Fraser. "For fans of the book, there are certain things that are so

iconic, and this moment is one of them," Moore relates. "The producers were very keen that we get mo-

"Initially, we filmed that scene where Bree's looking for [Jamie] and she actually runs past him and then almost has this sixth-sense feeling of, 'For some reason, I feel a pull toward that area,' and he's there. I wanted to play that bloodline pull, if you like, in terms of that sixth sense of seeing Jamie."

—SOPHIE SKELTON

"For that Claire moment, we had so many discussions about that. Knowing we couldn't do that scene as it was in the book, where Claire comes up and sees that Jamie and Brianna are sitting outside on the bench, we put a bench in Wilmington and had them sit there. That was our nod to, 'Okay, we didn't do it exactly like it, but this is our version of it.' I think it worked out really well."

—MARIL DAVIS

ments like this absolutely right. So it was really trying to work out with the actors and the cameramen how best to stage it to be as faithful as possible to the original source material. But in terms of the emotions, Sam and Sophie really knew, and understood, the importance of this. I thought Sam particularly played it absolutely beautifully. It was really, really gentle."

Moore acknowledges that Skelton had a much tougher job in playing that moment so soon after her character's assault. "[She has] to go from dead inside, then to this realization very quickly that it's possible that her mother and father are in town, then go and search for them. And then she discovers Jamie and there's a very emotional introduction to him. Obviously, she's hiding all this from her mother and father, so Sophie wanted to bury quite a lot of it. But every now and

again you need that in the performance for the audience to track where she's at. We gave ourselves the chance to do several takes and play with the performance."

Executive producer/writer Toni Graphia says Skelton really landed it when she falls into Jamie's arms. "There's so much there because we

know it's like a safe haven, in her father's arms, after this awful thing has happened to her."

The story then shifts to Fraser's Ridge, where Brianna acclimates to her new home while holding back on the truth about what happened to her, until Claire sees through her daughter's façade. "Claire knows

"Sometimes we use different stuff from the books from different places. We kept saying, what could they talk about [at the dinner]? Then we remembered that there was a story about Dougal warning Jamie about kissing his daughter that was way back in book one or two. We thought Brianna would want to know what Jamie was like as a young man. We pulled up that story and included it."

—Toni Graphia

her daughter enough to know something's wrong," Graphia details. "Bree had a very hard task, which is to play the joy of finding her parents and being reunited with them. But she was carrying the horror of the rape that just happened. You've got to put on a smile, and get along, and be happy, but your mom's going to see through you, because she knows you." When it

came time to shoot that sequence, Moore says, he just let two cameras run. "One was on Claire and one on Brianna and we let them go at it. Rather than do it countless number of times, we wanted to get the essence of the performance, them playing off each other and the shock of the revelation and see what that's like for the first time."

In turn, Jamie also takes opportunities to make his own relationship with his daughter. Graphia says, "We wanted our version where Jamie and Brianna just get to wander around the woods and talk, bond, and get to know each other in a really slow, heartfelt way. Sam gives great performances here in the way he looks at her and when he sees her smiling in her sleep."

Woven into those scenes was an adjustment from the book, where Bree originally asks Jamie what she should call him right when they first meet. "That should

have been earned a little bit," Graphia asserts. "So we moved it to later, to when Jamie lets her off the hook by saying, 'I don't hold anything against [Frank]. He raised a wonderful girl. And If I met him, I'd shake his hand and thank him.' Then she finally feels like she can call Jamie 'Da.' She doesn't want to call him 'Daddy.' She calls him 'Da.' And she has two fathers."

"I loved those scenes with Sophie, especially when we're picking the wild garlic and she tells me. It's just so heartbreaking. I'm not a mother, but I have younger siblings, and you have to draw on those feelings of wanting to protect people so much. Knowing that Brianna is now a woman, as her mother you can only just be there for her and hold that space for her."

—Caitriona Balfe

EPISODE 410: THE DEEP HEART'S CORE

Writer: Luke Schelhaas Director: David Moore

The secrets everyone's been keeping in the Fraser household finally see the light of day in the combustible episode "The Deep Heart's Core." As Claire had already learned of Brianna's pregnancy and rape in the previous episode, it was time for Jamie to find out. Co-executive

> *"I feel so fortunate working with an amazing actress, who throws herself into it and really connects to everything. Caitriona's a big friend now. I think that's the key and the magic to what you can create sometimes. We've been through so much together that it's really bonded us."*
>
> —Sam Heughan

producer/writer Luke Schelhaas says that long interaction between father and daughter proved to be a bold opening.

"The very early scene where Jamie and Brianna go for a walk and talk about what happened to her, she says, 'I wish I would have fought back.' He can't convince her

> "I had been looking forward to that particular moment since the beginning of shooting season four, because it was such a key moment in still letting Ian have his innocence. It was an incredibly organic moment. We got on set that day. [Sophie and I] had been joking about it, saying, 'Oh God, we're cousins!' I think we might have done it two or three times, and we just knew that we had hit the right tone, especially when I got the look off Caitriona as Claire of 'What the f*** do you think you're doing?' With that, I went, 'Okay, I've definitely hit the nail on the head here.'"
>
> —JOHN BELL ON IAN'S PROPOSAL TO BRIANNA

up talking about revenge and her sense that she'll never get over this. That was an important scene, taken largely from the book. And it was a challenging scene, just two people and seven pages long. I think it's a really powerful scene."

That interaction then gives Bree the strength to stand up against her well-meaning family and friends when she finds out they blamed, and banished, the wrong man for her rape. "We call it the scene where all cats come out of all bags," Schelhaas laughs. "It's the

that it isn't her fault, so Da does his unexpected, shocking thing where he fights her, pins her, and holds her to prove she could not have fought him. There's a lot more in that scene," he reveals. "They end

scene where she finds out that Roger was here and that Jamie beat up Roger. Then she goes and confronts Ian, and everything comes out, and everything goes wrong, and now the rest of the season is the search for Roger."

Director David Moore thought the scene, essentially played as one large ensemble in the cabin, was extremely successful. "This family, [despite] everything that's happened to Brianna, somehow bond and pull together emotionally for the most awful, tragic thing: Jamie thinks he's doing a good deed and gaining revenge and he doesn't realize he's beaten, and almost killed, the wrong man. One of my favorite scenes is where Brianna confronts Jamie, and Young Ian tells her what he's done and Brianna just punches him in the face. Every time I watched it when they were cutting it, I just roared with laughter, because she absolutely batters him, and he has got the most fantastic look on his face, with a bloody nose," Moore laughs.

At the end of the episode, Roger makes a run for it as his captors continue to push him on the

> "I understand that at the time they were the Iroquois, yet they were called the Mohawk tribe. Ian wouldn't call them Mohawk after his time spent with them. He calls them Kahnyen'kehaka, which is their word for their culture. Through meeting with the First Nations that came over from Canada, a lot of them had Kahnyen'kehaka as their bloodline. They have created a language preservation society in Canada, which is basically an online course that teaches you the basics of their language. I started with that because it was such a rich resource that I could dive into."
>
> —JOHN BELL ON LEARNING NATIVE AMERICAN LANGUAGES

> "It's very important to me to play the reality of something, to play something honestly. What would a man who has been through what he's been through and with the stakes as high as they are, out in the wilderness with a chance to save himself, do in a moment where it's all stacked against him? There's no perceivable way to get out of this situation, but there is one. You can play it as stoic, but I had to mark the breaking points. Anyone in that situation, I believe, would be horribly conflicted. The idea of saving himself is enough to cause something in Roger to break. It might feel like he's weak, even. I had considered that. It could be a perceived weakness in him. But at the same time, I thought, no, that's the truth of the thing."
>
> —RICHARD RANKIN ON PLAYING ROGER'S INDECISION

> *"I think the thought of Jamie's child being safe somewhere in the future would have been one of the things that Murtagh would have taken comfort in during the long years of indenture. Meeting her in the flesh brings out the fierce, protective side of his character. Working with Sophie is great, and so much happens to her that Murtagh, at times, feels a little helpless. There is also a definite sense that he sees her strengths as a Fraser already and admires her for that."*
>
> —Duncan Lacroix

road north to the Mohawk village. What could have been just a simple action sequence instead turns into a heartbreaking cliffhanger, as Roger stumbles onto a standing stone that could be his way home.

"There were some location-specific adjustments that we had to make, but that scene played out right as we conceived and wrote it," Schelhaas reveals. "That, to me, was a super-exciting sequence. I was so happy to be able to write that. His grueling escape, the slow-motion running, and then the surprise of those stones and the tie back to the first episode, where we see the stones being built eons ago."

"The art department did a fantastic job," Moore says of the created location. "Filming it, we used crane and drones. You're never quite sure what you'll get, because often what you want is all going through Roger's mind."

Schelhaas says Rankin's work elevated the whole sequence. "I don't think we scripted him saying her name. And the way he does that, he says her name and he steps back," the writer sighs. "I guess you do sense that he's going to touch it, but in fact he doesn't."

BUILDING SEASON FOUR:
THE MOHAWK AND CHEROKEE TRIBES

As the Frasers learn about their new home in America, they come into contact with the Native American tribes who are now their neighbors. As portrayed in Gabaldon's *Drums of Autumn*, the Frasers' interactions with the Cherokee and the Mohawk run the gamut from friendly to hostile, as their cultures coexist in a world that will gradually be obliterated for the Native Americans.

Knowing the complexity of that history, Starz and the *Outlander* producers made it a priority to portray the stories of the Native Americans in the series with authenticity. But Scotland, where the series had committed to remain for season-four production, is a coun-

try without a native pool of actors who could credibly hail from the tribes that populated the eastern portion of North America. To solve their problem, the producers and casting director Suzanne Smith looked to Canada.

"It was so important to us that we either cast Native Americans or First Nations actors in those roles," executive producer Maril Davis reiterates. "We knew we wouldn't be able to get everyone full Cherokee or everyone full Mohawk, but it was very important to us that they were indigenous people. We quickly realized that Canada was our best bet."

"It was really exciting that we had a great team for casting up in Toronto," producer David Brown explains. "We went all the way up into northern Alberta and into northern Toronto to find the people. We had such an amazing group of folks that came over, from various different groups and various different nationalities of the First Nations. It was fantastic. We embraced them, and they were fabulous people."

Hair and makeup designer Annie McEwan says that one of the prerequisites for playing an indigenous male role was to accept having a shaved head. While many of the younger actors had no problem, she admits selling that to some of the older gentlemen wasn't as easy. To bridge the gap, she says, "What we did for the much older guys is, we said once they're no longer a brave, they allow their hair to grow. There wasn't actually reference to [support] that, but there wasn't ref-

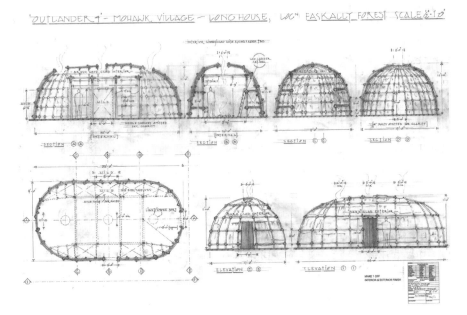

"I walked on to what looked, and felt, like a real eighteenth-century Mohawk village. It was almost like the mists of Avalon, or getting to do some actual time traveling. The costumes were amazing and so authentic looking. There was even smoke coming out of some fire pits and huts. The thing that really made the experience special was being surrounded be over one hundred First Nations Canadian actors and supporting artists. Some of the actors I knew and had worked with on previous projects, and some were household names that I grew up watching and was thrilled to be working with. There were some supporting artists who were from my home province and even some of Nakota heritage. It felt like everyone knew each other; at least we did through someone, and that we were all connected somehow. I don't think that the production could have known that this community feeling would be so present with First Nations people. Here we were, halfway around the world, representing a special culture and history."

—SERA-LYS MCARTHUR,
JOHIEHON

erence against it either. And a lot of the older guys didn't want to shave their heads, so that's the way we played that. We didn't have many. We had maybe about ten out of the hundred thirty actors."

Back in Scotland, creating the Mohawk village of Shadow Lake for the last episodes took the whole season to plan and execute. David Brown, Hugh Gourlay, Matt Roberts, and Jon Gary Steele scouted the rural locale for staging the fully environmental set.

Then production designer Jon Gary Steele went to work having his approved concepts actually built by the construction crew. "This was especially heavily researched," Steele explains. "And I have to say, it was quite fun; I've never built an Indian village before. It was built out in the middle of nowhere, near water, because we wanted to look out on it from the chief's longhouse. Luckily, the location had that, because I was gonna fight to get the money to build it up, because in the research, we found the chief's longhouse was built on a raised platform on a mound of earth so that it overlooked the whole [village]. And Stuart Bryce, the set decorator, found a place that built period-looking canoes. We wanted to see people coming up to the shore, out of these canoes."

To create the domed housing for the individual Mohawk families, Steele says, they individually hand-built them, based on the materials and techniques of the time. "[Our builders] would use small, thin trees, rip off all of the branches, and bend them to make the shape of these buildings," he details. "They're oval-shaped buildings, so they'd create the form, and then on top of that form, they would put the bark. We cast three different kinds of trees from the area to make plaster and fiberglass bark panels that would wrap around the whole thing. Then they did another set of all these bender trees that would go up and over the hump, so to speak, tied off with hemp. And then everything's aged with layers and layers of set dressing."

Stuart Bryce's team spent weeks researching the history of the Mohawks to get the right colors and details for the pieces that made the village look lived in and real. "We found two volumes of books by an artist called Robert Griffing," Bryce explains. "It was really difficult to find most of our research because of the time period. It was an etching, a painting, or it's the written word or some sort of artwork. Griffing had done this series of beautiful paintings of Mohawk, Cherokee, with lots of camp-life stuff. We didn't copy verbatim—like, for example, with the trade clothes and stuff, we

worked with costumes on that so that we were all running in the same color palette. We did slightly different designs, and we did lots of work with feathers and beads and wampum."

Using that as inspiration, they got to work making just about every

hand prop featured onscreen in the Mohawk episodes. "We outsourced some things—like we got some baskets from a couple who made us some birch buckets and little pots," he says. "And then from those, we took texture casts and made heaps of fake birch boxes, and then

"I am close friends with some Mohawk people, and even spent a few days on the Akwesasne reservation, which was the same nation where Outlander found its translator and cultural advisor. I knew some basic knowledge of their cultural practices and history, but was by no means an expert, as these tribal people differ greatly from my own people. I knew a few words and phrases, so it wasn't completely alien, but it was definitely very challenging. I was very grateful that Outlander had us working with their dialect coach Carol Ann Crawford, who was also the liaison between the Mohawk expert/elder, Eva.

"We were also given a PDF file of Mohawk cultural details that the Outlander production team assembled for us. Many of these cultural differences were highlighted in 'Providence,' such as how it is rude to point with one's fingers, but one should instead 'lip point,' as we say in Indigenous North American circles. It is also considered disrespectful to meet someone's gaze in many North American Indigenous cultures. This is a harder one to show in modern cinematic visualizations.

"I believe Outlander did a lot of due diligence and research into depicting the Mohawk culture, language, and people and I learned a lot while prepping for and filming this episode. I even got a tweet from a viewer who speaks fluent Mohawk, and she said she could understand everything I said in my scenes. She thanked me for doing my research and for representing the language accurately. This was the most treasured compliment of my work I received."

—SERA-LYS McARTHUR, JOHIEHON

we were able to manufacture hundreds of these little pots and buckets. All the tools they're using, all the little vases, the little girls' skirts, everything's all made by the prop department or the prop-making department or the drapes department."

"We even made tobacco," Bryce adds with enthusiasm. "We made tobacco out of paper. We ended up lacing really fine tissue paper with a latex solution that was pigmented, and we worked for months on that, trying to get the texture right, because tobacco is really fragile and difficult."

Meanwhile, McEwan and her makeup-and-hair team did their last-minute magic on the First Nations cast. "We had to dirty them down, and we were constantly try-ing to break them down to make them fade into the background once they were in their woodland. If they'd not got enough dirt and color on them, they'd jump out of all the green, so we had to just keep constantly throwing dirt makeup at them to just make them look like they'd been outside all the time. On the biggest shoot day, including my main team, there were probably thirty to forty makeup-and-hair people. Even for last checks, one person could only really fix the dirt on three of the actors in the big crowd shot, so we had to be on it all the time."

With weeks and weeks of detail work finally completed by all departments in time for the shoot, it was emotional to see all of it come together, Bryce says. "When the shooting crew were there, and when they populated it with all the actors and extras, with horses and dogs and all sorts of stuff like that, it was pretty special to see these people acting in this environment that we created in Scotland. You don't often get a chance to create something like that."

David Brown adds, "When I saw the First Nations folk coming in to that village the first time, that really struck a chord of pride, because they were just so amazed by what we'd done as a production in terms of putting it all together. Everybody was really excited by that, and that makes the heart grow warm. The hidden joy of that is Gary and I found that [location] way back, seven months before we started filming it."

EPISODE 411: IF NOT FOR HOPE

WRITERS: SHAINA FEWELL AND BRONWYN GARRITY

DIRECTOR: MAIRZEE ALMAS

With Brianna ensconced at River Run while Jamie, Claire, and Ian travel to the Mohawk to find Roger, "If Not For Hope" gives Brianna the opportunity to understand the dire circumstances she now lives in as an unmarried, pregnant woman in the 1700s. Jocasta is determined to do right by her niece by getting her married off, which creates a cultural, and personal, impasse for the two women.

Producer/co-writer Shaina Fewell says the writers were interested in exploring whom Brianna considers an ally or not. "Bree is exploring her relationship with Jocasta. It's about when you're starting to understand that your biological family is different than the family that you knew for so long and what that does to a character as she's going through these hard times."

Without family to turn to for help, Brianna goes to the man who is like family to the Frasers, the vis-

iting Lord John Grey. "A part of the book that I really liked is the relationship between Lord John and Brianna," Fewell says. "There's some really challenging stuff that they have to go through, for Bree in particular. It was exploring the difference between their characters in the book and then seeing these actors take on these roles and [figuring out] how these two people are going to end up getting engaged. It's

> *"John's a hero of the interpersonal most of the time. He's not the guy you see on the battlefield correcting things, like Jamie. He's much more adept at relationships and maneuvering them. He's a master at that. That's his stock-in-trade, in terms of his heroics."*
>
> —DAVID BERRY

a reminder of everything they've gone through before we get into this really heavy stuff that we're gonna fall into for the end of the season."

As Bree finds herself pressured to pick a suitor, she makes some desperate choices that aren't entirely fair to Grey. "We all had lots of heated debates and conversations in the [writers'] room about the fact that she was going to black-

"When Brianna proposes to him, he's definitely caught off guard. It's characteristic of him to then proceed on his good nature, which more often than not puts him into situations that he struggles to keep on top of. It's very hard to do the right thing in the Outlander world, and it's very hard to know what the right thing is to do. But John is guided by compasses wanting to do the right thing all the time. And so he then agrees to marry Brianna."

—David Berry

mail John Grey," Fewell admits. "It's an iconic part of the book and something that's so exciting but that has to be earned, because you don't want to end up in a place where she seems cold. You need to understand the duress."

Joining the debate and guiding the visuals was well-known genre-television director Mairzee Almas (*The 100, iZombie*), who says she had real sympathy for Bree. "In her journey, she's had to look at it and say, 'What's the most important thing here?' Then it's to make the decision that the most important thing is her baby and to survive."

As production kismet would have it, the very first scene on Almas's first shoot day was the scene where Bree poses the engagement arrangement to John. "Usually with these big, pivotal scenes, you want it a little deeper into the episode, but we had a chance to chat about their fears or concerns. It's a pretty simple scene, in that she's taking him away from prying eyes and ears and she's presenting her plan. She needs privacy to do it, but we also wanted the production value that *Outlander* is known for and [to] see the plantation in the background. The environment is now a character in our show, and I contextually wanted to put it between them in the frame."

Closing out the episode, Jamie and Claire have a moment of rec-

onciliation on their trek as they forgive each other for their parenting failures with Bree. "We did spend a lot of time in the room talking about what it means to have a child," Fewell says of the scene's origins. "How you can have this relationship where you totally understand each other but the child really will add a new dimension, which is exciting and powerful but it is challenging. This is their time to learn how to communicate and be parents together and what that means overall to their relationship. One of my favorite parts about exploring that mo-

ment, and it was one of Bronwyn's too, is that we both have kids, so we both got to really explore what that means in life, and for us, and for friends. Even though we're in the 1700s, it's definitely one of those relatable moments that is timeless."

In creating that poignant moment, Almas says, the tight space inside the tent didn't make it easy but she wanted to capture that almost confessional sense. "Claire's speaking about Brianna and her safety, and Jamie, unbeknownst to Claire, is feeling the guilt of everything," Almas details. "Their

noses are pointing in different directions. They just are not connected. But we also want to know that these two love each other very, very much, and that they have already gone through so much for each other. The scene treats both the characters honestly and allows us to have a male character, Jamie, being really open and talking of honesty. Maybe it's a terrible generalization, but I think that it's very refreshing for women to see a man be really honest about his insecurity and not pretend to be the guy that's in charge of everything."

SPOTLIGHT

NATALIE SIMPSON AS PHAEDRE

As the Frasers become accustomed to the Americas in season four, the narrative allows Jamie and Claire to experience the full spectrum of what the colonies represent—the good and the bad. Jocasta Cameron's River Run plantation is the perfect microcosm of opportunity and oppression. As a single-woman landowner, she's challenging the patriar- chy already firmly entrenched in this New World. But she is also a slave owner, and her prosperity as a tobacco farmer comes on the backs of others. The series doesn't shy away from the issues, allowing audiences to experi- ence them through the eyes of new characters like Jo- casta's maid Phaedre.

British theater actress Natalie Simpson took on the

character knowing that the supporting role would be representative of a terrible institution woven into America's history. "I felt a lot of responsibility in creating someone that was three-dimensional," she shares. "I was very aware that I was playing someone who was living out a daily horrific situation. Secondly, I wanted to commit to showing that this person had other sides to her, and this person could be happy, excitable, and silly. She could do all of those things living in a world which was against her. It was difficult because I wanted to show the reality of what it was to be a slave in that time, but I also wanted to show the other side. So I spent a lot of time trying to find that in the beginning scenes that I had. It was incredible to be a part of that, because I think that did come across—the horror of it but then the tiny moments of love and life."

As one of Jocasta's house servants, Phaedre lives a discreet existence from those who toil outside the main house. "I spoke to Colin [McFarlane, who plays Ulysses] about how we felt about it and how we wanted to hold ourselves," Simpson reveals. And she says she spent a lot of time figuring out how Phaedre and Jocasta would interact with each other. "Because Jocasta's blind, she can't see me, so how cheeky can Phaedre be? Knowing what her situation is but also knowing that she and Jocasta do have quite a relaxed, for those times, and informal relationship. It was fun trying to figure

that out with Maria [Doyle Kennedy] and Caitriona [Balfe]."

As with most life experiences, you can prepare as much as possible but being in the moment is often totally unexpected. Despite being a member of the Royal Shakespeare Company and finding comfort on the boards, Simpson had never worked on a TV series before *Outlander*. "The scene with Claire and Jocasta, that was my first day on a TV set," she says with awe. "The lynching at the end [of 'Do No Harm'], that was my second day ever on the TV set. I've never been in this world, and the first thing I did when I walked on set was I just cried."

Overwhelmed, as both a fan of the series and an actor getting her first big TV break, Simpson admits it was an experience she'll remember forever. "With the lynching scene, I was a roller coaster of emotions because it was genuine. I didn't have to do much acting for that," she says somberly. "The supporting actors were amazing and they were bringing all that they had. I felt really intimidated as a person being in that environment, and it was intense. So it was a baptism by fire, but I really liked and was proud of the way that it came across. And I watched the episode with my mom and my sister, and we were like debating and it was great. I felt proud to be a part of it."

The strange necessities of film and TV production

often mean actors will leave the filming for some time before they are needed again. Simpson was in that position playing Phaedre, who, after "The False Bride," wasn't needed in the narrative again until "If Not For Hope."

"I shot those [first] two episodes in October, November-ish time, and I wasn't back again until the spring of the following year," Simpson explains. "But when I came back, they were so lovely and they gave me big hugs and were like, 'Welcome back,' so I slipped back into it. You just have to train your brain into dropping right back into it. But I have a lot of amazing people to watch and learn from."

Simpson particularly liked having scenes with Sophie Skelton's Brianna when she came to live in River Run. "From Phaedre's point of view, I think she's just unbelievably excited to have a young woman around," the actress posits. "Someone that she can dress, someone that she can chat with, and someone who is as relaxed and welcoming as Claire. I think she sees [Brianna]

as another version of her and warms to her instantly and cares about her, as she can see that she's going through something. I think she almost lives vicariously through [Brianna]. She gets excited when she might be engaged to someone and [is] meeting men. Phaedre just gets excited and tries not to think about her own life and maybe projects onto her a bit."

Brianna also gives Phaedre the gift of acceptance, which is beautifully played when Bree sketches her. "Phaedre spent her whole life really looking after other people and putting the attention on them," Simpson says. "I think she got so shocked by someone noticing her in a way that no one really had before. I don't even think Brianna knows what she's done, just treating her like a normal girl. Phaedre hasn't ever had that, so I think it's a really lovely relationship. Phaedre's light, and fun, and cheeky, but I think it's good to remember what it is that she's living. In moments like that, you can see it seep through—where her head is, how she feels about herself, and the world that she's in."

EPISODE 412 : PROVIDENCE

WRITER: KAREN CAMPBELL DIRECTOR: MAIRZEE ALMAS

In "Providence," after being dragged up-country for weeks, Roger finally arrives at the Mohawk village of Shadow Lake in upstate New York. Meanwhile, at River Run, Brianna finds out that Bonnet is being held in prison and she enlists Lord John's help to get some closure.

Even though they can't know it, both are seeking absolution for their souls.

> "In the book, the Mohawk village is called Snaketown. We were told by our American Indian advisers that it was actually quite offensive to them because they don't name towns or villages after animals and the snake is a bad omen. We had to change that name to Shadow Lake."
>
> —MARIL DAVIS

For Roger, his captivity by the Mohawks ends up as an evolving array of humiliations. From his failure in the gauntlet to his lowly place in the camp, Roger is a beaten man until he's placed in confinement with fellow exile Father Alexandre Ferigault (Yan Tual). "It was tricky," co-producer/writer Karen Campbell says of portraying their stories. "In the source material, you have so much more time to exam-

ine characters. So, for me, what was fun was having Roger be in a place where he has suffered so much that he's like, 'This love stuff is bananas,'" she laughs. "He is just done. He has chased Brianna through space and time, only to, arguably, get raked over coals. And once you are ready to throw in the towel, something happens that then makes you realize, 'I can't quit this person.' It was really fun to challenge that character."

> "We did an additional day for the exploding of the jail because we had to pull that exploding jail out of our hat. The special-effects guys had like two days to do it, as it changed from something else."
>
> —MAIRZEE ALMAS

Returning director Mairzee Almas says her time working in the created village and with the First

Nations actors was a highlight of her career. She says the work of David Brown's and Jon Gary Steele's teams was jaw-dropping. "Right now, even talking about it, I'm welling up, because these First Nations people were just so beautiful. I mean, honestly, it was so touching."

That authenticity all around allowed for the tragic story of Father Alexandre and Johiehon (Sera-Lys McArthur) to be an effective life-changing motivator for Roger. "We

"It's very touching when Jamie writes Brianna a letter. He's trying to teach her about pain and about how to come to accept that revenge is going to eat you up inside, how you should let it go. I think it's hard for her to understand that. But it's wonderful that he gets to be a father, in a way, and have an impact in this very powerful moment."

—SAM HEUGHAN

really wanted to make Johiehon feel like a real character, so that when she does walk into that pyre, she's not just some cipher," Campbell says. "She's kind to Roger because she is the healer of this tribe. However, she also fell in love with an outsider, with Father Alexandre."

Despite Roger's cogent and vulnerable pleas to the priest, he can't stop Ferigault from his path of self-punishment, which culminates in his burning on the pyre and Johiehon sacrificing herself too for

their love. Though the shocking outcome is also featured in the book, the writers wrestled mightily with keeping it. "The idea that this woman loves this man to such a degree that she's willing to die with him to seal their fate in an afterlife together was something that I thought was so metal," Campbell says.

Almas admits she had a harder time with the idea of any mother leaving her child behind. "So how I ended up finding my peace and my love with it was I took away the Brianna and Roger of it, and the Jamie and Claire of it. Now we have these lives, these hopes, these dreams, these souls, that are so entwined that no matter what we do to try and disentangle [them], they cannot. They cannot live without each other. And then we tried to echo and show these repercussions through the other relationships."

Campbell continues, "Roger, seeing this woman sacrifice herself to be with Father Alexandre, he's like, 'I do love Brianna and I would

do that for her,' and that gave him some clarity. And Mairzee Almas directed that beautifully. That final sequence is just heart-wrenching, which is what we intended it to be."

In Brianna's narrative, she travels to Bonnet's jail so she can act on

"We did tons of research and found a jail somewhere on the east coast [from] the eighteenth century. It was now a museum made of yellowed wood. What was fascinating about it was each window had these giant straps of metal, not just bars, across [it]. We did more research on it and it was because, back then, people would use a horse and wagon and pull the bars out of windows to help their friends escape. So we did like three feet of metal straps that go beyond each side of the window. It's not explained, but it's there."

—JON GARY STEELE

"Our stunt people were awesome, but it was still a nail-biter, because essentially we had one shot at doing that beat where our stuntwoman steps up to be with the stuntman [on the pyre]. We had one shot because the reset on it is so long because everyone's wearing flame-retardant clothes. We had to make sure it goes as great as it's gonna go, because we know we have one bite at that apple."

—KAREN CAMPBELL

Jamie's recommendation of freeing herself through forgiveness. Another controversial decision to portray, writing the sequence was tricky. "For me, personally, sexual assault is something that is unforgivable," Campbell asserts. "As a modern person, it's very challenging to wrap your head around some of these older ideas. So what was important, at least, was to track Brianna's emotional journey through the episode. She knows this is something that she wants to do but that it's terrifying, and there is anxiety around it. It should feel hard for her."

Almas says they also wanted to show that Brianna's choice is a reflection of the time she comes from. "She's a woman of the seventies that's looking at this going, 'I'm trying to have a healthy way to move forward.' And if she births the child and it looks just like the rapist, will she be able to love this child? She needs to make this child an innocent and not a reminder."

Campbell continues, "I think Ed and Sophie did a great job in that scene. Sophie also did a lot of research, and she and I talked about the weight of something like this. When he says, 'I'll be gone but not forgotten,' she turns on him and unloads that she will never tell the baby about him, and that to me feels like a moment where she takes back some power. She can't change what he's done to her, but she has zero intention of remembering him in any meaningful way, so essentially he will be forgotten."

SPOTLIGHT

JOHN BELL AS YOUNG IAN MURRAY

While only in his early twenties, actor John Bell is well acquainted with the pressures of taking roles in projects with intense fan scrutiny. Bell's first acting gig was in an episode of the granddaddy of all beloved sci-fi series, *Doctor Who*, and he was a character in Peter Jackson's *The Hobbit* film adaptations. However, when an audition for *Outlander* came his way, the actor was unaware of what he was potentially embarking upon.

"I'd heard of the show, but I hadn't really known how big it was," Bell admits a bit sheepishly. "So for me it was quite the adventure right at the beginning, getting to go online and research the whole character, research his story. I was blown away by his arc throughout all of the books, so I was definitely raring for the audition and really, really hoping it would pay off."

Bell says he did the work on his interpretation of Young Ian Murray for the audition and soon after learned that the part was his. Bell's first appearance as Jenny and Ian Murray's son was in "A. Malcolm," where he's incredulous at his introduction to his long-lost auntie Claire.

Bristling from the rules laid upon him at Lallybroch, Young Ian runs away to stay with Uncle Jamie. Bell was told to lean into Young Ian's youthful exuberance and impulsiveness. "We started with a story of Ian being a little bit petulant, a little bit selfish. Thinking that his life—despite a quite privileged life for eighteenth-century standards—was not enough for him. His idea of the world was one that was very romantic. I think it goes back to when he's talking to Jamie about his days in the war and how he's almost longing for that. Jamie's the one that's telling him that

> *"John Bell is so lovely as Young Ian. Young Ian is so endearing, but he's also slightly—in a humorous way—a thorn in Jamie and Claire's side sometimes. We definitely play around with that dynamic a little bit, which adds some needed levity. It's always fun because we definitely tease John Bell too, because he's the new kid on the block. It was lovely to see progression, though, as well, him maturing and becoming this young man. It was a lovely, different way of exploring motherhood this season."*
>
> —CAITRIONA BALFE

war isn't romantic, but still, nothing really dismays Ian, which is a part of his character I really enjoy playing. He's incredibly brave and resilient."

Looking for adventure and to make his own way in the world, Young Ian has no idea that Claire's return will jump-start his coming of age as a series of circumstances—including being kidnapped by pirates—befalls him. "Very quickly, he is rushed from being this naïve and innocent boy into this really dark, dangerous world that immediately I was drawn to, because it can show such a development of character," Bell says.

To play out his character's arc, Bell traveled with the core cast and production crew to close the season's shooting in South Africa. "Being on location together, we were relying on each other as a big family more so than ever before, and that's where I really got to have time, not just with Sam and Cait, but also with my other fellow supporting

actors, like Lotte [Verbeek] and Lauren [Lyle] and César [Domboy]. I think that was the turning point for me when it came to feeling like I wasn't just a character on the show; I was part of the clan. I was part of the Frasers," he finishes with a smile.

"It was also at that time that it dawned on me, the gravity of what people were expecting from the character, because he's a favorite to many people," he continues. "I had maybe a little bit of nervousness from thinking that, but when it went out onscreen, the majority of people absolutely adored what I was doing, so I kind of felt that that was the final point at which I was like, 'Okay, I feel comfortable now. I feel ready to do this.'"

Bell's confidence carried him into season four of *Outlander*, which is a big year for Young Ian as he starts a new life with his aunt and uncle in America. "What was nice about the fact that the season started three months after the events of season three [was] that Ian—especially in my head—was spending even more time with Jamie and Claire," he says of building backstory for Ian. "They are like his second parents in this New World.

"I mean, Claire gives him a hard time at points, but he's always ready to take it, because he loves her so much," he laughs. "And what I love about Ian is that he listened to his auntie Claire and he's so proud of her. I think that comes across in some of his lines—like evidently she's spoken to him about the Native Americans, so when he's like, 'The Native Americans were here first, were they no?' that was a really modern viewpoint for a white colonist. That was a really nice moment to show the effect Claire has had on him. And then with Jamie, [he's learned] this idea that a man's worth is not predetermined by what happened to him but by what he chooses to do."

At Fraser's Ridge and River Run, Young Ian soaks up everything he can learn about this new land and in turn continues to explore who he wants to be as he grows into his adulthood. In particular, Bell says, the sequence when Ian and Jamie beat Roger without mercy for Brianna's assault is a moral turning point for his character. "Ian suddenly becomes very complicit in a very violent choice by Jamie, and I think there's a key line where Jamie says, 'Get rid of him,' and Ian's right there with, 'Should I kill him?'" the actor says solemnly. "I don't think Ian would have said something like that in season three, you know? So we're already seeing this darker possibility within him."

However, Bell points out that the flip side of that dark impulse is made right when Young Ian overrides his uncle and volunteers to take Roger's place in the Mohawk village. "Since we first introduced him, we've been building toward that moment when he is standing in front of Jamie," the actor explains. "That's why it was so important to have that scene at the beginning of the season where Jamie was comforting him, because the tables have turned. Now it's Ian comforting Jamie, tell-

ing him, 'I will not forget. I am doing this and I am saving you. Take this chance and leave me; I will survive. I've proven to you now that I can survive.'

"Ian is searching for respect from others in this season," Bell continues. "He's searching for respect from Jamie, and then he searches for respect from the Native Americans. Like, I think it's beautifully done when the young Mohawk, who is the mirror image of him in the

tribe, pushes him into that gauntlet, and at the end he's there cheering him on. So it also comes down to learning to respect himself and his own decisions and choices. For me, that's his core moment in that season—he is learning to respect and find that inner strength."

While that moment brought many in the audience to tears, Bell says that he was hit even harder seeing the final cut of Young Ian standing next to the Mohawk chief. "The smile that comes across his face is just one of absolute joy," he says with pride. "I was nearly on the verge of tears at that point too, because that was the proof of the pudding. He'd done it; he'd succeeded."

Bell admits it was quite the arc to play in one season, but he's come out the other side even more excited for how the series will frame Young Ian's future stories. "I thoroughly enjoyed having to play his innocent, cheeky, comedic, fun-loving side up until this point. But now I think that side of Ian is being left behind in his childhood. It's all in the eyes now—he's dealt with so much trauma and so much pain that he can never go back to being that same kid who dreamed about what it would be like to fight in a battle, because now he's fought his own battles, and he's very aware of the price of it."

EPISODE 413: MAN OF WORTH

WRITER: TONI GRAPHIA DIRECTOR: STEPHEN WOOLFENDEN

"Man of Worth" found executive producer Toni Graphia closing out the season as a solo writer, with first-time *Outlander* director Stephen Woolfenden translating the page to screen. A second-unit director on huge films like the *Harry Potter* and *Fantastic Beasts* series, Woolfenden was well versed in helping land epic narratives, but he admits it was still daunting. "It

> "It'll be interesting to see where [Jamie and Brianna] go now. Obviously, there's this unspoken [idea] that Jamie has betrayed her in a way, almost killing the man that she loves. And now Jamie wants to do everything he can to right that."
>
> —SAM HEUGHAN

was a one-off finale that needed to tie up *a lot* of loose ends in the

whole series," he states. "It's such a big emotional arc—tying up Bree's story and putting the family back together was the center of my task."

Woolfenden started his directorial duties with seven days of shooting in the Mohawk village to close out that story line. "That proved to be such a wonderful thing, as it was key to getting everybody together," he details. "It really created a sense of company. We got

all the wonderful First Nation Americans and we had these big, emotional scenes about how the village is portrayed, letting the actors do their work. My big task was to get everybody together and say, 'You've got to feel connected and you've got to be part of that village.' Everybody responded to it." And, he adds, "the weather was good!"

"'Man of Worth,' as a title, was planted way back in 'America the Beautiful,' when Ian wants to stay and Jamie says, 'I want you to be a

> *"When I go up to the final chap and I'm tackling him, I slit my thumb open on his costume. I was like, 'What would Ian do in this moment? He would keep going!' With the blood pouring out of my hand, I kept going with this scene, making sure that when I got to that final moment, the blood is in the shot, so they know how much I worked for it!"*
>
> —JOHN BELL

man of worth,'" Graphia reveals. "Now Jamie has to be a man of worth to make good on his promise to his daughter; Roger has to be a man of worth and decide whether to come back and stand by his wife; and Ian is a man of worth, trading himself with Roger and righting that wrong."

In those last Mohawk scenes, Woolfenden was also especially thrilled with how Young Ian's arc played out. "Those performances between Sam, Cait, John, and Rich-

ard really set the groundwork emotionally for the episode. You just knew the weight of everything at stake there. Those performances surprised everybody, because they absolutely took them near to a level where everybody was feeling what they were feeling and it was so strong and it was about family."

The culmination was the gauntlet sequence, this time run by Young Ian. "John Bell must have done it twenty-five times," Woolfenden says with admiration. "I had three cameras on it: one on a crane, a Steadicam, a handheld. He was so revved up for it and ready to go. It was very exciting, and it went pretty smoothly. There was that lovely jewel at the end of the gauntlet, when he succeeds in getting to the end—he has that smile on his face, with the shouting and the scream-

ing at becoming part of the Mohawk. We just let the cameras run, letting that adrenaline come out of him. It just happened naturally and that's real."

As with all finales, there was a lot of redrafting to figure out the best alchemy of ending certain stories and then tipping up where the narratives will go in season five. Graphia admits her first draft included the Scottish Gathering that is a big set piece in the fifth book, *The Fiery Cross*. "I jumped way ahead, and then I realized it wouldn't all fit," she laughs. "So then we went backward and focused on 'Where's Roger,' and decided to show him come back."

Shockingly, Graphia ended up paring back too much. "This was the first and only episode I've ever written that came in short," she says

with a smile. "Matt and I are always arguing because I write very long episodes. Some of my first drafts will be ninety pages. And I always get the phone call of 'What the heck are you thinking? You gotta take twenty pages out of this.' I don't know what I was doing in this finale, but somehow the script was only like forty-two pages. This was the first time I got a phone call from Matt that said, 'Hey, I know this seems crazy, but I'm asking you to add scenes.'"

As a result, we see more Murtagh and his romance with Jocasta in the finale. "He wasn't even in there, so that was our very, very last-minute decision," she reveals. "We thought we would do a slow rollout [with Jocasta], where they would clash a few times, and butt heads, and then gradually fall in

> *"Jamie sees this fire in Roger, and he knows that by allowing him to take it out on him physically, it'll guide past that emotion. And hopefully they can come to a new understanding. It was just a great scene to have, and quite a long day. It was a very tense scene and we had to do it over and over. Richard was so strong in those moments. He enjoys that physical stuff with Jamie—a real strop. Jamie really wears all his scars on him. He's constantly ready to put himself forward and has to stand up for things that he's done and accept responsibility. I think it's the beginning of the understanding between him and Roger."*
>
> —SAM HEUGHAN ON THE JAMIE AND ROGER FIGHT

love. But when we put them together, we thought, 'Let's just jump them right into bed!' She throws whisky in his face, and, boom, they're in bed, so that we could move forward with the story. And we came up with the thought that instead of falling in love, which is different than the book, that Jocasta has always been in love with him, but he wanted her sister."

Romance also comes into play

when Roger arrives at River Run and Brianna sees him from her window. "I'm a big romantic at heart, so that sequence is all about scale and heart and energy and desire," Woolfenden explains. "I asked Sophie, 'Can you run in your costume, on this hot day, from the door over to him?' She did beautifully, with the same energy every time. It looked good. It felt good. When you saw her running toward camera, everybody was very, very excited."

For the very last scene, the original idea was going to be a giant cliffhanger. "Claire and Jamie get home, and Brianna says, 'Where is Roger?' And cut to black." Graphia smiles. "But we didn't want to leave Roger hanging out there for a whole droughtlander, with fans thinking that he didn't come back to Brianna. We thought that would be very unsatisfying. So then we decided on the letter from Tryon. We always knew that season four was about Jamie's deal with the devil and that Tryon was the devil.

"The choice was made that [the birth] became part of a music sequence so you don't really hear her screams, but her screams were incredible. We had a medical adviser there, and that was a real birthing stool from that period that she was sitting on. I just liked the fact that everybody's trying to help and it shows Bree in her most determined. She's going to do this and nothing's going to stop her and this is not going to be a horrifying experience. It's going to be a real, human experience, and she's going to survive."

—STEPHEN WOOLFENDEN

Now Roger has returned, and then, boom, the letter comes. It's a real cliffhanger that allows you to start [season five] wherever you choose to. But, if you start right from that moment, there's *a lot* to still have to deal with."

"[Jocasta's bedroom] is a softer place; the draperies and the bed always help with that. It's got to feel like it fits in that house, so it's still quite dark. We found that beautiful embroidered silk, and we put panels on the walls. We complemented that with the bedding, so it's really quite simple but a subtly beautiful space."

—SET DECORATOR STUART BRYCE

CONCLUSION

LOOKING FORWARD

If you're a fan of Diana Gabaldon's *Outlander* books, then you know that as of early 2019 there are eight novels that already exist about the Frasers, their ever-expanding family, and a network of supporting characters. But in the world of television adaptations, there's no guarantee that any series will exist in exact parity with its source material. Which is why *Outlander* fans were so thrilled to learn on May 9, 2018, that Starz had picked up the series for seasons five and six, each with twelve episodes, to adapt *The Fiery Cross* and *A Breath of Snow and Ashes*.

Knowing the show was secure in its future, with a deep bench of loyal executive producers to guide

it, Ron Moore officially stepped back from day-to-day involvement at the end of season four to develop new series. "I knew that in subsequent seasons, I would delegate more and more, and I would let some of the other people take the reins. I think it has a lot to do with the way I was mentored and came up in the business. I spent the first ten years of my career at *Star Trek*

and I was allowed to move up through the ranks, from a freelance writer, literally in every writer title, all the way up to co–exec producer by the end. It just felt like this is a good way to do it and it's nice to be able to give that back. Now Matt Roberts is definitely running the show at this point," Moore says with pride. "I'm just seeing story outlines and scripts, but after he's done the initial work."

And executive producer Maril Davis is still committed to the *Outlander* day-to-day, even as she develops new series with Moore. "While I'm not a writer, I try to spend a lot of time in the writers' room," she explains. "It's helpful for me. As a creative, non-writing producer, I can't always stay

on a show day to day for this long. Your focus becomes split with other projects. But this one is close to my heart. I'm dreading the day the show ends because I love this one so much. I enjoy all the projects, but some are more special than others, and this is one of them. I just love our crew, I love the content of the show, and I love the actors."

The writers and producers started work on adapting season five in the fall of 2018, picking up the story threads that were left as tantalizing cliffhangers for the audience. Davis says playing all of that out is still deeply exciting to the creative team. "You have to think ahead. These books are not stand-alones. They do continue and, as a TV series, you do have to think about it. You want some momentum going into next season, and how we leave off here affects that next one."

Season five certainly leaves the core characters in places of extreme vulnerability. "Roger comes back to Brianna, but it takes him a few days. They have this joyful reunion, but what are the ramifications of that going to be?" Davis teases. "Brianna has been victim to a rape. There's so much stuff there. Obviously, we brought Murtagh back, and once you bring a character back, it changes everything. A lot of people I know talk about whether or not we replace him with the [book] character Duncan Innes, which we're *not* doing."

Instead, the series is fully com-mitted to exploring what Murtagh and Jamie being on opposite sides of the Tryon conflict means to the story and to their bond as family. "It's something we're obviously going to plan in season five," Davis continues. "The idea for Jamie is that he's finally gotten his family back together; he rescued Roger. Yet it's not over. Here's another situation, so it just keeps piling on for him."

In the end, the *Outlander* faithful wouldn't have it any other way, because there's nothing more inspiring or exciting than watching how Jamie, Claire, and their family overcome what fate and destiny throw at them, with love, persistence, and pure Scottish stubbornness.

OWN SEASON 4 ON COLLECTOR'S EDITION BLU-RAY™

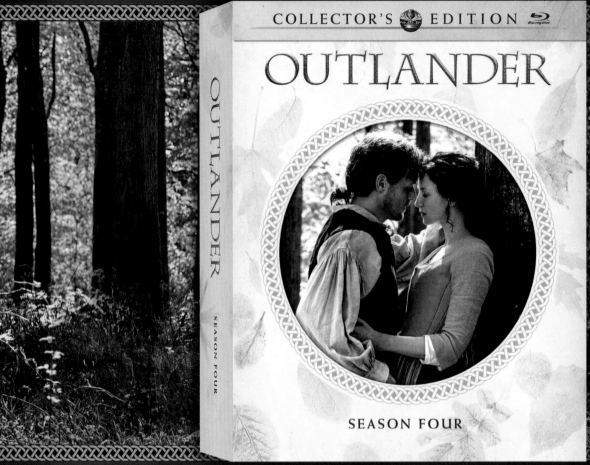

COLLECTOR'S EDITION

OUTLANDER

SEASON FOUR

Includes an exclusive 28-page book, 4 *Outlander* Untold bonus scenes, Season 4 soundtrack, & a sneak peek from Diana Gabaldon's *Go Tell the Bees That I Am Gone*

ALSO AVAILABLE ON BLU-RAY™ & DVD

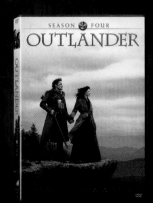

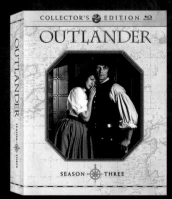

NOT RATED

© 2018, 2019 Sony Pictures Television Inc. All Rights Reserved.
© 2019 Layout and Design Sony Pictures Home Entertainment Inc. All Rights Reserved.